JUSTICE
IN
MODERN
SWEDEN

Tänka Fritt är Stort
Men Tänka Rätt är Större

To think freely is great
To think rightly is greater

Motto on the Administration Building
Uppsala University, Sweden

JUSTICE IN MODERN SWEDEN

A DESCRIPTION of the Components of the Swedish Criminal Justice System

By

HAROLD K. BECKER, D.Crim.
Director, Center for Criminal Justice
Professor, Department of Criminal Justice
California State University, Long Beach

and

EINAR O. HJELLEMO, M.S.
Visiting Professor, Department of Criminal Justice
California State University, Long Beach
Retired Detective Chief Inspector
Oslo Police Department
Oslo, Norway

CHARLES C THOMAS · PUBLISHER
Springfield · Illinois · U.S.A.

Published and Distributed Throughout the World by
CHARLES C THOMAS • PUBLISHER
BANNERSTONE HOUSE
301-327 East Lawrence Avenue, Springfield, Illinois, U.S.A.

© *1976, by* CHARLES C THOMAS • PUBLISHER
ISBN 0-398-03486-9
Library of Congress Catalog Card Number: 75 19254

With THOMAS BOOKS *careful attention is given to all details of
manufacturing and design. It is the Publisher's desire to present
books that are satisfactory as to their physical qualities and artistic
possibilities and appropriate for their particular use.* THOMAS
BOOKS *will be true to those laws of quality that assure a good
name and good will.*

Printed in the United States of America
N-1

Library of Congress Cataloging in Publication Data

Becker, Harold K
    Justice in modern Sweden.

    Bibliography: p.
    Includes index.
    1. Criminal justice, Administration of Sweden. 2. Police—Sweden.
3. Corrections—Sweden.
    I. Hjellemo, Einar O., joint author. II. Title.
HV8231.B4   364   75-19254
ISBN 0-398-03486-9

This book is dedicated to our wives, Donna and Stella.

FOREWORD

By Donald R. Cressey, Ph.D.
Professor of Sociology

SMALL IS BEAUTIFUL. A Swedish automobile manufacturing company—small in comparison with Ford or General Motors—produces a small car so fine it competes successfully with American behemoths on their own turf. More generally, the small Swedish nation has a quality of life envied by the national giants.

Although the sources of this effectiveness and happiness are not easily identifiable, they clearly seem related to the Swedes' enviable ability to debureaucratize even their largest bureaucracies, public and private. As the authors say in their concluding chapter, "Participatory management in private companies by members of the labor force, as well as lay judges, lay element on probation boards and local police councils, and political representatives on the policy-making boards of the national administrative agencies, reinforces our perception of Sweden as a firm democratic bastion."

Sweden's system of criminal justice is noted for its repeated demonstrations that to be big is not necessarily to be better. For example, the National Correctional Administration has shown that prisons can be desirably local and autonomous while at the same time fusing into a national and regional organization. Further, this centralized bureau has shown that a decentralized small prison whose total population consists of twenty men can more efficiently, justly, and beautifully do things to, for, and with prisoners than can sprawling prisons designed and administered on the assumption that mass production processes and procedures are signs of efficiency, justice, and beauty.

The recent (1965) conversion of local Swedish police units into what amounts to a national department similarly managed to avoid rigid bureaucratization despite increased bigness, urbanization, and industrialization. Centralized administration has not demolished the intimate and beautiful relationship between police and public that stems from smallness. Local chiefs of police remain responsible for keeping the peace in their own communities, but their work is coordinated, and they can get assistance when they need it.

A Stockholm police officer who is a friend of mine actually experienced the nationalization of the police as decentralization. Just after the administrative change, he expressed enthusiasm for his work under the new arrangement, which he had opposed. When I asked him to describe his work, he said his new assignment was "to be a policeman." He was not being evasive. He had been ordered to go into a neighborhood and do good police work—along any lines he thought appropriate. Like any other true professional he was allowed to keep his own time schedule, so he worked days, nights, or split shifts, as he deemed proper and efficient. When he went to work—sometimes on Sunday, sometimes in the middle of the night—he sometimes donned his uniform and he sometimes did not. The officials of the new National Police Board, like his local department chief, trusted him to keep the peace, and he did. Perhaps, when all is said and done, it is such conditions of trust that make smallness so beautiful.

This small book itself validates my thesis that smallness and goodness go together. It is not a study in "comparative criminology." It is not even a detailed report on a study of the Swedish Criminal Justice System. It is a short description of how the Swedes are organized to do many things so beautifully. Consequently, it is itself beautiful.

University of California
Santa Barbara, California

May, 1975

ACKNOWLEDGMENTS

AN INTRODUCTORY TEXT to Swedish criminal justice cannot be expected to present all the background data that have an input on crime control and law enforcement. However, a modest presentation of the principal features of Swedish society and government has been attempted. While we would appreciate all the facts that might have a bearing on the evolution of a society's institutional framework, practical considerations advise us that a selection of social indicators will guide us in forming a reasoned opinion on how this nation has matured and regulated its external and domestic environment.

The authors wish to express their gratitude to California State University at Long Beach for its assistance in developing a four-week criminal justice foreign study program in Sweden which was offered for the first time during the summer of 1974. Many thanks to the University of Uppsala, Sweden's oldest university, located forty-five miles north of Stockholm, which was host to the study program.

Also, the authors would like to personally thank The Swedish Institute which made much of its information on Sweden available to us and the National Police Board for its permission to include organizational charts and other material in our text.

H.K.B.
E.O.H.

CONTENTS

JUSTICE
IN
MODERN
SWEDEN

CHAPTER 1

INTRODUCTION TO SWEDISH CRIMINAL JUSTICE

For some years Sweden has attracted considerable interest, not only in the United States of America but in a number of other countries as well. It has even been suggested that Sweden be looked at as a laboratory for innovative social and political reforms.

> Sweden has the most advanced and complex system of public administration based on ministries. In Sweden it was held that the joint control of administrative services and policymaking would lead to tyranny. The new constitution of 1720 specified, therefore, that members of the Council of the Realm (policy direction) could not be members or heads of the administrative boards (collegia). The only exception to this rule was the chancellor, and it is from this office that the modern prime minister has descended. The presidents of the administrative boards were specially appointed and protected from detailed interference from the Council of the Realm. The reason for this is a pronounced dualism in the Swedish system of government. The political direction of the country is in the hands of the cabinet assisted by the staffs of the different ministries. The bulk of administration is the responsibility of about sixty royal boards. Every ministry, except the Ministry of Foreign Affairs, has a number of these boards attached to it.[1]

Attached to the ministry of justice, for instance, are the National Police Board and the National Correctional Administration. They are funded by the ministry subject to the approval of the national assembly. However, they display considerable independence and have some statutory powers. Each board is headed by a director general assisted by members most often comprising legislators. Neither the government nor the national assembly have any direct authority over the boards.

As to political ideology one scholar has asserted:

> American youth looks upon Sweden with envious eyes. Here is a society which has combined socialism and capitalism with considerable

3

success. Sweden has managed to stay at peace when all around it the world went up in flames. Sweden has made advances in extending its social services and boosting its standard of living beyond previously known boundaries. It has preserved its traditional values while seeking new freedoms, thus combining tradition and progress.[2]

To suggest that the Swedes have solved critical problems of crime control would be pretentious. However, efforts to adjust smoothly to changes in social patterns and to keep abreast with scientific research have long been recognized. Introducing a study on the Swedish response to crime, American Chief Justice Warren E. Burger has stated the following:

We can afford to take a hard look at all our institutions, compare them with other societies, and learn from them as they have so often learned from us. The contrast between our programs and those in some of the countries in Europe, the Scandinavian countries in particular, is not a happy one for us. Countries such as Sweden have long engaged in research on lawbreakers and prisoners, and on anti-social conduct generally. The Swedes use a wide range of institutional treatment and extensively employ work release and open prison techniques. Their use of psychological testing and psychiatric counseling and therapy is far in advance of ours.[3]

The aspect of crime that has caused most anxiety in recent years has been the individual and collective violence, commonly associated with competitive urbanized societies. There are indications that violence is widely regarded as instrumental in both maintaining social control and producing social change. Meanwhile the following observation should not be ignored:

"Contemporary events in the prosperous countries of Western civilization leave no hope, unfortunately, that violence can be checked simply by making available to all greater wealth and physical comfort. Even a country as prosperous and economically well organized as Sweden is not immune to the problems caused by violence."[4]

It is probably fair also to include critical attitudes. After spending eleven years in Sweden a reporter for *The Observer* in London has written:

Sweden, as few will now need to be reminded, is the epitome of the welfare state; the model of affluence, where poverty is outlawed; the Mecca of the social engineer. It is egalitarian, orderly, well run and most efficient. The real power lies in the hands of the party bosses, the bureaucrats and the trade union leaders—who together form an impregnable ruling establishment. There is an intolerance of independent thought. Deviation from the collective opinion, the consensus, is now regarded as among the worst of crimes. Saddest of all, this "tyranny of the compact majority"—as the Norwegian playwright Henrik Ibsen once put it—has been promoted by the media.[5]

COMPLEXITY OF THE COMPARATIVE APPROACH: Successful governments rarely display much interest in external comparative research for the purpose of improving their own institutions. When things go bad, however, criticism becomes vocal, and the structure and functioning of human institutions come under scrutiny. This is when organizations look outside their own national frontiers. A better method, of course, would be ongoing comparative information and solutions prior to potential problems.

Even if methods and techniques embrace a wide substantive range, the problems of the practical world tend to determine the relevance of the subject matter. Currently, comparative studies, research, and analyses, particularly those using a cross-cultural approach, are fashionable.

The American record of devising solutions to technological problems is universally recognized. Admirable, massive research to trace the origins and causes of crime, however, has proved frustrating. Crime in modern Western democracy appears too complex to solve with the methods and tools currently available. With the fundamentals of American social control, its ideology, and constitutional guarantees left untouched, concentration has been on personnel and equipment, with approximately one billion dollars allocated annually by the federal government in these areas.[6]

While not rejecting social experimentation, it is probably a fair statement that the trend of causal crime research is rapidly declining. The focus is on how the social institutions can be improved. While many human institutions have universal characteristics, different cultural environments have produced institutions of varying structures, functions, and viability.[7]

One point should be stressed: namely, that modern political systems based on government by consent, private property, and enterprise still constitute an acceptable basic framework within which social policy can be resolved. Along a political system continuum this encompasses a range from limited government to a sharing of means and goals between private enterprise and collective endeavor. A second approach is to view the criminal justice system as a function of the political system, which requires an interdisciplinary academic approach.[8]

Interest in Swedish society can be credited to the reputation of Swedish institutions, artists, and scholars. Well-known names in recent years include Alfred Nobel's prizes in peace and scholarly achievement: Gunnar Myrdal, the political economist; Dag Hammarskjöld, late secretary general of the United Nations; and Ingmar Bergman, the movie director. A survey of mass-media coverage in the United States shows that Sweden attracts more interest than the other Nordic countries combined. When the obsolete term Scandinavia is used, Sweden is thought of most of the time. A summation of Sweden is most poignantly stated as "What Scandinavia does today others will do tomorrow."[9]

In order to set the scene some geographic, demographic, and social indicators may serve as illustrations. Sweden covers 175,000 square miles, approximately the size of California or twice the size of England. It is Europe's fourth largest country in area after Russia, France, and Spain. It occupies the same latitude as Alaska but enjoys a temperate climate thanks to the Gulf Stream. Sweden has the world's lowest child mortality rate with 11.1 deaths per 1,000 of all births. The Swedes read more newsprint than any other nation with approximately 534 publications per 1,000 inhabitants. The average consumption of hard liquor per capita is 5.2 litres compared to 5.7 in the United States. The number of cars per 1,000 inhabitants is 291 in comparison to 446 in the United States. The gross domestic product per capita is 5,880 dollars compared to 6,260 dollars in the United States—both are above all other nations in the world.[10]

Without deserving the label of state capitalism, Sweden has long practiced economic planning as a means of reaching the egalitarian road. The economic policy aims at eliminating excessive wealth and poverty. Subsequently, the steep progression in taxes appears harsh. But financially, the Swedes and resident aliens are protected from the cradle to the grave. Slums like Harlem and Watts are conspicuously absent.

From a criminological point of view the preoccupation with Swedish suicide rates is intriguing. Statistics show that 1,648 Swedes committed suicide in 1973—that is, 22 per 100,000 population compared to 1,332 in Los Angeles County—or 19 per 100,000 population. Los Angeles County has a million fewer people than Sweden. Overall, the life span for Swedish men is eight years longer than in the United States and for women, four and a half years longer.

In the following papers the structure and the functioning of the criminal justice system, the contribution of the political and cultural environment, and the way some serious manifestations of deviancy in other countries have been contained, will be examined.

FOOTNOTES

[1]Brian Chapman, *Profession of Government: The Public Service in Europe* (London: Allen and Unwin, 1959) , pp. 18 and 49.

[2]Alvar Nelson, *Responses to Crime: An Introduction to Swedish Criminal Law and Administration* (South Hackensack: Rothman and Co., 1972) , p. iv.

[3]*Ibid.,* p. v.

[4]Rene Dubos. "Biology, Society and the Individual," *Dialogue,* Vol. 7, No. 1, 1974.

[5]Roland Huntford, *The New Totalitarians* (New York: Stein and Day, 1972) .

[6]Einar O. Hjellemo and Harold K. Becker. "Sweden 1974: A Comparative Experience in Criminal Justice," *Journal of California Law Enforcement,* Vol. 9, No. 3, January 1975, pp. 115-120.

[7]*Ibid.*

[8]*Ibid.*

[9]G. B. Baldwin. "Population Policy in Developed Countries," *Dialogue,* Vol. 7, No. 2, 1974.

[10]1972 figures; dollar estimates based on 1 SKr (Swedish Krona) equal to approximately twenty-four cents (1974) .

CHAPTER 2

CRIMINAL JUSTICE SYSTEM IN ACTION

POLICE BY VIRTUE OF THEIR ROLE in social control make daily decisions pertaining to the preservation of peace, regulatory law, and crime repression. A public consensus can hardly be expected in all cases. When persuasion and mediation fail, physical coercion, as a last resort, is usually undertaken.

The preservation of order is a fundamental political responsibility without which no systematic economic activity and meaningful social interaction are possible. In modern democracy the parties contending for power may differ much in their views as to the kind of social peace and conformity they want. Governments by popular consent expressed through general elections meanwhile tend to demonstrate that the electorate judge political programs by results rather than by intentions. In the exercise of police powers moderation and the avoidance of extreme measure to maintain order, as well as the credibility and moral support, are tests of political maturity.

Neither too much nor too little force should be applied in order to preserve or restore domestic order. Excessive use of violence creates public indignation and reduces the moral acceptability of political authority. Inept or insufficient coercive power discredits authority by undermining public confidence in its ability to govern.

This dilemma is sometimes brought to the fore by spectacular events.

EXAMPLE 1—THE NORRMALMSTORG BANK ROBBERY: In the autumn of 1973 Sweden held a general election for Parliament. The incumbent cabinet had sprung from the social-democratic party that had held government powers for some forty consecutive years. Electoral campaigns made the incumbent officeholders vulnerable to attack, more particularly so if some incident could be exploited to blame the government. As in several other countries law and order is a sensitive issue.

Thursday, August 23, 1973, provided sensational headlines for the mass media: An armed suspect had barricaded himself in a bank vault with hostages, following an attempted bank robbery. The suspect, later identified as having a long criminal record, had been interrupted by a police patrol car and had fired at it with a submachine gun. The public could view what has been called the *dramatization of evil* on the television screen and read detailed accounts in the newspapers, while the suspect was still in the bank.

The incident occurred at ten o'clock on a busy morning in the Creditbank at the Norrmalmstorg, a square in Stockholm that has given its name to the incident which was to last for six days. Alerted by an alarm device the police ordered patrol and detective units to the scene. A detective walked into the bank and urged the gunman to surrender. The response was a volley of shots which wounded the detective in the hand. He was taken to a hospital. The suspect, whose face was disguised, took a number of bank employees as hostages after he fired more shots to terrorize the victims.

Requests made to the gunman to surrender proved futile, and a siege was prepared. The police commissaire heading the squad dealing with violent crimes managed to negotiate with the suspect who demanded the following: a ransom of half a million dollars, the release from prison of a convict friend of his, and safe conduct out of the country.

The political authorities had to decide.

The minister of justice agreed to release a convict named Olofsson (26 years old, serving a life term for murder) in return for the freedom of the hostages. After a while three hostages came out, but it appeared that the suspect retained six additional hostages.

The convict was driven to the bank and joined the unidentified gunman, and the ransom money was delivered. The erratic behavior of the gunman caused the police to call in psychiatric expertise. Other persons working in the building were evacuated while the negotiations continued.

A fast car was parked outside the bank as requested by the suspect. A new attempt to get face-to-face contact resulted in more shots being fired, hitting a second police officer. However, the police succeeded in limiting the siege to the bank vault area after two more hostages escaped.

The police drilled a series of holes through the ceiling and started pouring in sleeping gas. Again the gunman defied the police and damaged a drill with explosives. Cords placed around the necks of the remaining hostages by the suspect might strangle them if they lost consciousness, and the sleeping gas was subsequently abandoned. Also, an attempt to put drugs in the food brought to the vault was rejected.

Police sharpshooters wearing bullet proof vests and gas masks could not neutralize the gunman because of his closeness to the hostages.

The police had checked on all prison furloughs and believed the gunman was Jan Erik Olsson, who had failed to return to prison after his furlough. The police chief of Stockholm finally decided to spray teargas into the vault, and ambulances with medical personnel were summoned. The dramatic publicity of the incident had caused concern because the gunman listened to the radio.

The teargas shocked the gunman and within minutes he handed over his submachinegun. Police officers moved quickly and brought out the hostages, one of whom had to be carried on a stretcher. The criminals were led away in handcuffs.

The prime minister, who had been continually informed of the details, also had suggested solutions. He now rushed to the scene accompanied by the director general of police. At 10 P.M. on Tuesday, August 28, 1973, he publicly praised the police for the calm, patient, but determined and nonviolent handling of the critical task of securing an armed criminal.

It was, of course, a costly operation: An average of more than 100 police officers were on duty at all times during the six-day siege. The worldwide publicity in text and pictures devoted to the incident focused on the persuasive persistence of the police as contrasted to the shoot-outs that are too frequent in many other countries. Complimentary statements were offered by major international newspapers.

While some of the decisions had political overtones, the leadership of the operation comprised of police, firemen, physician, and forensic, psychological, and psychiatric personnel. A German police psychologist praised this combination when making comparisons with the disastrous happenings during the 1972 Olympic Games in Munich.

Because of the outcome in Stockholm little opportunity was left for partisan political exploitation during the ongoing electoral campaign.

A thorough analysis was undertaken by a committee summoned by the police chief. Statements showed that the suspect had boasted to the hostages of his previous crimes and, significantly, enjoyed telling what he had learned from an American movie on the subject of a robber who used hostages. The report was disseminated to police chiefs in various parts of the world who had requested information on what deserves the label, *an appropriate lesson in social defense.*

EXAMPLE 2—CRIME ADJUDICATED BY CITATION OF ON-THE-SPOT FINE: Serious crimes, usually called felonies in common law countries, are processed through the courts of law by the Public Prosecution Authority.

In Sweden, however, fines are by far the most common approach to criminal behavior with over 300 crimes being adjudicated by citation of on-the-spot fines. Approximately 95 percent of all persons found guilty of violating penal and regulatory law are fined.

If the violation can be defined as an infraction, the patrol and traffic officers are authorized to issue a writ (Förelägg) describing the unlawful behavior and to impose a fine. This can only be done if the suspect is more than fifteen years of age, acknowledges the deed, and accepts the fine which is regulated according to a tariff prescribed by the director of public prosecutions. A citation form is subsequently signed by the police officer on the spot and handed to the offender who has a time limit for payment by mail or check. The maximum fine for one infraction is approximately 60 dollars and for several infractions, 96 dollars. If a person is eighteen years of age or younger and is charged with drunkenness in public in conjunction with other infractions, the police officer cannot issue a citation. Normally, such cases are referred to the Alcoholic Care Service.

The vast majority of infractions pertains to road traffic and parking. The Swedish term for the fine is *Ordningsbot*. The police officer cannot receive any cash payment. Cases subject to on-the-spot fines must be clear-cut. The fault must be readily admitted by the offender. In case of doubt the matter is referred to the local state prosecutor. Any fine that has been accepted by the offender has the legal status of a court sentence. If the offender requests advice from parents or a lawyer, the police officer will grant this, but no movement from the location is permitted. The offender's name is not included in the criminal records but is filed at the local precinct and destroyed after four years.

The most recent on-the-spot instructions were issued by the National Police Board in December 1974 and comprise over 300 prohibitions.

When considering the principle of separation of governmental powers, some might object to executive officers being entrusted with what appears to be an adjudicating function. The practical advantages meanwhile are considerable, such as allowing the court machinery to move faster. Pursuant to the Swedish Code of Judicial Procedure of 1942, there are three types of monetary penalties: (1) a sum of money, (2) an amount computed as day-fines (introduced in 1931), and (3) on-the spot fines. Day-fines were introduced to adjust the amount to the financial situation of the offender. The maximum day-fine per day is 120 dollars. When computed according to days the upper limit is 14,400 dollars. If the fine is not paid within the specified time, the penalty is converted to no less than ten days and no more than ninety days in jail. Pursuant to an agreement between the Nordic countries in 1963, any person can be made to serve the sentence in the country of his citizenship. Fines can be imposed by a court as well as by a public prosecutor. The forfeiture of goods as well as public fees can be imposed in connection with fines. Payment by installments is often granted. It is rather surprising to note that more than 90 percent of all fines imposed are actually paid.

EXAMPLE 3—THE INTOXICATED DRIVER: An important subject of regulatory law in our automotive society pertains to traffic safety. Conclusive analyses have verified the relationship between the intake of liquor by drivers and the risk of accident involvement. A survey by the World Health Organization has shown that by the time an alcohol concentration of .08 percent (based on 100 mg per 100 ml) has been reached, this influence emerges as the dominant factor in determining the risk of accident involvement. In the United States it has been claimed that traffic deaths every year average 55,000, exceeding the total American loss of lives in the Vietnam War: 45,941. In Sweden since 1925 insobriety while driving a motor vehicle has been unlawful.

In 1943 the penal provisions against drunkenness on the road were included in an Act of Parliament with amendments as recent as 1957. In Sweden a person who has an alcohol content in his blood of 0.15 percent (150 mg/100 ml) or above is considered unfit to drive a vehicle. He is liable to imprisonment of a maximum of one year with the suspension of his driving license, as a rule, for two years. If the blood concentration amounts to 0.05 percent (50 mg/100 ml) or more the penalty would be a fine or imprisonment for no more than six months. Suspicious drivers are stopped and are subject to a breathalyzer test given by the police. If the test is positive, the driver is brought to the nearest police station, and a medical doctor is called in to take the blood test which is made compulsory by law.

Admittedly, tourists visiting the country are not always acquainted with the law. A businessman from Kuwait, who one Sunday evening in the autumn of 1974 drove a car in downtown Stockholm, was checked by a police patrol. He smelled of liquor, and the police officer administered a breathalyzer test. The color reaction of the pretest was unmistakable, and the tourist was brought to a police station nearby for the extraction of a blood sample. An alcohol content above 0.15 percent (150 mg/100 ml) was revealed by the forensic laboratory analysis. The offender had rented a car in Stockholm, and he consumed a few glasses of beer in a restaurant in Kungsgatan. Unacquainted with Swedish traffic law he had thereafter driven downtown. He was on a short visit to Sweden and was not involved in an accident. In view of the situation the tourist received a fine. Because of his wealth the maximum amount was imposed by the city court. This was the first time in

Sweden that any court had applied the maximum fine of 120 days at 120 dollars per day or 14,400 dollars.

The Nordic countries reputedly have the most severe drunken driving regulations in the world. Research has not solidly verified the deterrent effect of these laws. On the other hand it has not been empirically documented that the Swedes refrain from drinking liquor when they are driving because of the legal prohibition.

Whatever may be said about the moralistic attitudes reflected in some Nordic laws, any legislation on road safety will be ineffective if it is not enforced and if the penalties are not appropriate.[1] This was dramatically demonstrated when the new Road Safety Act went into effect in England October 9, 1967. Vigorous law enforcement probably accounted for a major part of the 22-percent reduction of traffic deaths during the first four months compared to a similar period in 1966 and 67. The percentage of accidents involving drunk drivers is lower in Sweden than in most comparable countries. Mitigating circumstances like the one reported above are rare.

The ordinary reaction to a first time offense is one month in prison. Repetition of the violation results in the withdrawal of the driver's license forever.

EXAMPLE 4—THE SECURITY POLICE.[2] A matter that has aroused great public interest in Sweden pertains to the activities of the Security Service which is jointly vested in the Surveillance Branch of the National Police Board and the Security Division of the Military Defense Staff.

The task of the Security Police is to prevent and expose offenses which constitute a threat to the national security of Sweden. This function includes the collection, compiling, and processing of intelligence material which is necessary for judging and countering an attack against the outer and inner security of the country.

Another of the duties of the Security Police is safeguarding Sweden against infiltration.

The Security Police also keep a special intelligence file which is regarded as an indispensable instrument in its efforts to prevent and discover offenses. The register is primarily an aid in police work. It also provides information in connection with personnel control. This type of control consists in the collection of particulars from the file regarding any person who has been, or will be, taking up a post of significance for the security of the country. The National Police Board is allowed to record information necessary for the work of the Security Police. It is prohibited, however, from making an entry solely on the grounds of a person's political views or membership in organizations.

The Swedish Defense Staff has a special division which is responsible for security matters and is assigned the duty of creating safeguards within Swedish Defense against activities threatening the security of the country. This division is not, however, allowed to keep its own information file on persons whose reliability is open to question. Such a register may only be kept by the Security Police.

Time and again the Swedish mass media have reported assertions to the effect that the Security Police keep records of persons contrary to the above-mentioned prohibition of registration solely on the grounds that a person belongs to an organization or has in some other way declared deviant political views. It has also been asserted that the Security Division of the Swedish Defense Staff keeps a special file for recording data on persons with particular political opinions, despite the fact that this is forbidden. The assertions on unlawful intelligence information are very strongly worded.

In the light of this situation, the ombudsman carries out a very extensive inquiry into the matter. He has access to documents of both the Security Police and the Defense Department, classified and nonclassified documents which could have relevance to the issue. He interviews a great number of high officials in defense and in the Security Police. These include the supreme commander of Swedish Armed Forces, the chief of defense staff, and the head of the security division of the defense staff. The ombudsman also holds hearings with practically all the chief officials of the Security Police, including the chief commissioner of police, the chief of security police, and the lay representatives on the National Police Board, all of the latter being members of the *Riksdag* (Parliament).

As a result of the inquiry, the ombudsman can report that the assertions made regarding the registration of political views by the Security Police are groundless. Another finding of the inquiry may be that no register of political views was kept by the security division of the defense staff.

Reference is often made to the military industrial espionage case involving Colonel Wennerström. The minister of justice in 1966 stated that, "Under such conditions it is as impossible not to apply this form of defense of our democratic society, as represented by the Security Service, as it is to ignore our military defense in order to reserve our neutrality. It is simply a question of democracy's right to self-defense."

By comparison, the Federal Bureau of Investigation only has statutory authority for domestic intelligence. In 1947 the American federal government established the Central Intelligence Agency authorized to deal with external intelligence and expressly prohibited from exercising police, subpoena, or law enforcement powers, or internal security functions. Its role was to protect the external safety of the country. During the winter of 1974 to 1975, the American public with consternation read that members of the CIA had been unlawfully engaged in domestic spying aimed at political dissidents. The gravity of such clandestine operations was emphasized when the president ordered the secretary of state to obtain the facts while the Senate Armed Services Committee initiated hearings. Soon after, several officials of the CIA unit entrusted with this domestic activity did resign their positions.

In contrast to Sweden, which has a predominantly homogeneous population, the United States is a pluralistic society. By tradition the American government has been generous in granting asylum to a variety of political refugees, as well as displaced persons. Experience has shown that some of those persons have abused this generosity by being disloyal to their new homeland. Heterogeneity, a large population, and an extensive territory have exacerbated the domestic security problems. The FBI's intelligence operations apparently were not felt by the CIA to be sufficient, since the latter assumed some surveillance of potential subversion. The fact that this topic was examined by both Sweden and America demonstrates the sensitivity and the importance of the matter in a democratic society.

FOOTNOTES

[1]J. D. J. Havard. "Road Traffic Accidents," *Who Chronicle,* Vol. 27, March 1973. World Health Organization, Geneva.

[2]Adapted from the Annual Report of the Swedish Parliamentary Ombudsman for 1972. (Stockholm: I. Häggström AB, 1973), pp. 655-656.

CHAPTER 3

CULTURAL BACKGROUND

S WEDEN IS A LAND OF PARADOX: The state religion is Lutheran, but only about 7 percent of the population attend church; there is a monarchy, but the King has few powers; there has not been a war for 160 years, but a standing military force is maintained.

To attempt to understand the Swedish criminal justice system, one must first look at some of the components which make up in part the cultural environment of Sweden.

DEMOGRAPHY

POPULATION: The population of Sweden is slightly over 8 million people about 3 million of whom live in the three largest cities and less than 2 million in rural areas. There are 3.1 million households, 1.1 million of them with children under sixteen years of age. Women outnumber men in the towns, particularly in certain industrial areas, but are far outnumbered by men in most agricultural areas. About 40 percent of the married women work full- or part-time outside the home. Most of them, however, live in urban areas and either are childless or have children of school age. In the largest cities, more than 50 percent of married women work.

The country has a low birth rate and a slow rate of population growth. A considerable part of the country's population growth since World War II has been the result of net immigration. About 400,000 aliens live in Sweden, nearly half of whom are Finns. Foreign labor has been essential to industrial expansion.

There are about fifty-two inhabitants per square mile in Sweden, but they are very unevenly distributed. More than 90 percent of the population lives in the southern half of the country.

Sweden has a Lutheran state church, of which all Swedes are members provided they have not formally withdrawn.

GEOGRAPHY AND CLIMATE: Sweden is the largest of the Scandinavian countries and the fourth largest in Europe, 174,000 square miles. Slightly over half of Sweden's land area is covered by forests; less than 10 percent consists of cultivated land.

HISTORY

Sweden entered history with her far-reaching trading tours during the seventh and eighth centuries. In the ninth century, these tours took on a more warlike character when Nordic Vikings ravaged widely in the Christian countries of Europe. Swedish Vikings even traveled down the Russian rivers and as far as the Black Sea and the Caspian Sea. During the eleventh and twelfth centuries, Sweden gradually became a unified kingdom, which later included Finland. Christianity made its breakthrough, and Sweden received its first archbishop at Uppsala, in 1164. In 1397 Queen Margaret of Denmark united all the Nordic lands into the Kalmar Union which in the fifteenth century gradually led to open conflict between the Swedes and the Danes. The Union's final disintegration in the early sixteenth century brought on a long-lived rivalry and a series of severe wars between Denmark-Norway on one side and Sweden-Finland on the other. These conflicts broke out time and time again and left deep marks in the history of the Scandinavian countries.

Gustav Vasa crushed the attempt to patch up the Kalmar Union in the early sixteenth century with his fight for an independent Sweden. He carried out a number of penetrating reforms and laid the foundation for modern Sweden. At the same time he broke with the Catholic Church and drove through the Reformation. In the seventeenth century, thinly populated Sweden-Finland with scarcely more than a million inhabitants emerged as a great power after victorious wars against Denmark, Russia, and Poland; and its contributions during the Thirty Years War under Gustav II Adolf (known in English as Gustavus Adolphus) determined the political, as well as the religious, balance of power. After Sweden conquered several provinces from Denmark in 1658, Swedish-Finnish power embraced present-day Sweden, Finland, Ingermanland (in which Leningrad is now located), Estonia, Latvia, and important coastal towns and other smaller areas in northern Germany. With some reason, Sweden could demand that the Baltic Sea be regarded as a private, Swedish-Finnish inland sea.

Russia, Saxony-Poland, and Denmark-Norway pooled their power in 1700 and attacked the Swedish-Finnish empire. Although the young Swedish king, Karl XII (also known as Charles XII), won spectacular victories in the early years of the Great Northern War, his plan to attack Moscow and force Russia into a peace proved too ambitious. During a siege of a Norwegian fort in 1718, Karl XII fell in battle. In the peace treaties which followed, the allied powers, who were joined by Prussia and England-Hanover, put an end to Sweden-Finland as a great power.

Later, as a result of Napoleon's alliance with Russia, the eastern half of the kingdom, Finland, was lost (1809). However, Sweden's contributions under the newly elected crown prince, Karl Johan Bernadotte, in the war against Napoleon were recognized at the Vienna Congress, and Sweden received compensation in that Denmark was forced to give up Norway, which was then united with Sweden. The Sweden-Norway union lasted until 1905 when it was peacefully dissolved at Norway's request.

Popular government in Sweden rests upon old traditions. The Swedish Parliament stems from the ting (tribal courts) and the election of kings in the Viking Age. It became a permanent institution in the fifteenth century. Today, Sweden has a parliamentary government built on a party system. The Social Democratic Labor Party has been in power since 1932, practically without a break. The monarchy is constitutional and the king's authority is of a purely formal nature.

The impact of the Industrial Revolution was not felt in Sweden until the latter half of the nineteenth century. Rapid population growth at the same time was relieved partly through a huge migration of about a million Swedes to North America. Thus, serious overpopulation problems did not arise. The change from an agricultural to an industrial country took place without violence or upheaval. The long peace since 1815, the lively demand for Swedish raw material and products, and the absence of more serious social problems lie behind the economic well-being that is characteristic of Sweden today.

Swedish belongs to the Nordic branch of Germanic languages. Swedes, Norwegians, and Danes can make themselves understood by each other because their languages are similar. In Finland there is a Swedish-speaking minority.

SOCIAL LIFE

CULTURAL LIFE: Cultural institutions are largely government-subsidized. A guiding principle of the government in this regard has been to spread these institutions and their activities throughout the country, since in geographical terms cultural events and access to cultural life are unevenly distributed in Sweden. Attempts have therefore been made to create traveling theatre groups, orchestras, and exhibitions. Theaters are also trying to reach new audiences by giving performances at schools and places of work. Writers and artists receive support in the form of scholarships and guaranteed annual income.

Radio and television are operated as a monopoly in Sweden by a semigovernmental corporation, on the basis of an enabling agreement with the government. There are three parallel radio networks and two television channels.

Public libraries numbered 598 in 1972 and owned a total of 27 million volumes. In that year 2 million people took part in study circles arranged by voluntary adult education organizations receiving central and local government subsidies.

THE ECONOMY: The preliminary central government budget for the fiscal year 1973 to 1974 was approximately 16 billion dollars (one Swedish Krona equals approximately 24¢). Of this amount, 34 percent comes from direct taxes and 56 percent from indirect taxes. Of total expenditures 29 percent goes to social welfare programs, 16 percent to education, and 12 percent to defense.

Table I presents the distribution of the labor force between economic sectors and indicates the structural changes which have taken place within the Swedish economy during the past decades. Most evident is the reduction in the agricultural population. But this has been compensated for by a very considerable increase in agricultural productivity. The extent of Swedish agricultural production is determined politically; by a parliamentary decision, the

Justice in Modern Sweden

degree of agricultural self-sufficiency, which in the early 1970's was about 85 percent, will be lowered to 80 percent by the close of the decade. Swedish agriculture is protected against competition from abroad, and Swedish food prices are therefore higher than world market prices. Most agricultural production takes place on small family farms, but the farmers are, for purposes of selling their products, organized into producers' cooperative organizations.

TABLE I

PERCENT OF LABOR FORCE BY ECONOMIC SECTORS

	1930	1950	1972
Agriculture	36	20	7
Mining, manufacturing, and construction	32	41	37
Commerce, transportation, and communications	18	24	21
Public administration and other services	6	11	35
Others	7	4	0.1

The industrial population has ceased to increase and started to decrease as a result of a high degree of industrialization which during the past decade has carried with it a considerable trend toward mergers, especially in export industries. Most Swedish industry is privately owned. In the mining and manufacturing sector private corporations cover about 90 percent of production, while cooperative and public enterprises are responsible for about 5 percent each.

The most striking change has taken place due to the sharp rise in the employment percentages within public administration and other services. This is also reflected in the share of Gross National Product (GNP) which is related to public services: It has increased from 20 percent in 1950 to 32 percent in 1972. A growing share of GNP goes for investment: in 1972 the figure was 22 percent; public investments in that year amounted to 38 percent of all investments.

INCOME: The normal income of a male industrial worker in 1972 was between 6,480 dollars and 7,200 dollars a year. Many families receive extra income from the wife's earnings or from secondary employment. All children under sixteen years of age qualify for a tax-free government family allowance of $317 per year.

A study allowance of 216 dollars a year is paid to the parents of every boy and girl who pursues education past the age of sixteen. Students at university or college level qualify for further government support, in the form of both grants and loans, which in 1972 totaled 1,193 dollars per semester (a half year). This amount varies since it is tied to the cost-of-living index. Allowances are also related to the beneficiary's income or net wealth or, if the student is married, to the income or net wealth of the spouse. The income or net wealth of a student's parents is not taken into consideration. The loans fall due when the student begins earning income from work, with installments starting three years after the last examination and finishing not later than his fiftieth birthday.

In the white-collar sector, a business executive may earn an average income between 18,000 and 24,000 dollars a year. If both husband and wife are working, the total income may be 24,000 dollars or more. Before 1965 married couples were taxed jointly and thus counted as one income earner. Between 1965 and 1971 they had a choice of joint or individual taxation on income from work and of employment or self-employment; and starting in 1971 all income from work has been individually taxed.

HOUSING: The most common sizes of dwellings in Sweden are two rooms plus a kitchen in a rented apartment and three to four rooms plus a kitchen in an owner-occupied unit. Rented apartments in a new building will normally cost $2.40 to $2.88 per square foot in a large town and $1.68 to $1.92 per square foot in a small town. Rents are lower in older buildings than in those newly constructed, but the trend is toward greater equality in costs. The annual cost of a larger family house (5 to 6 rooms) may run between $2,880 and $3,600 if located near a city, between $1,680 and $2,400 if farther out. These figures are very approximate, since costs will naturally vary according to local amenities, building standards, and inflation.

Families with children under sixteen years of age and with limited income can get government housing allowances, and in most communities there are also local housing allowances. The size of government allowances depends on the number of children and the size of income, and there are certain requirements regarding minimum standards of dwelling. The lowest allowance is 173 dollars a year for a family with one child and an income of about 5,280 dollars; the highest is 922 dollars for a family with five children and an income of about 9,600 dollars a year. The local housing allowance is tied to the size of the rent, or to the operating expenses of owner-occupied houses; and its function is to cut off the top part of extremely high housing costs for families with lower incomes.

EDUCATION: Nine years of schooling are compulsory for all children, starting at age seven. Additional education is available at secondary schools offering twenty-two different fields of specialization. Some of these courses are two years in length and provide vocational training in fields such as the garment industry, business, or engineering. But only by completing certain three-year courses at a secondary school can students enter a professional college or one of the country's six universities. In 1972 there were about 123,000 college and university students in Sweden, of whom 40 percent were women. About 90 percent of the sixteen-year-olds go on to pursue at least two years of secondary education, and in recent years 25 to 30 percent of the twenty-year-olds have been enrolled in post-secondary education. Schools and universities are run by central or local government. In primary and secondary schools instruction and books are free of charge, and a free lunch is generally served.

WAGES AND LIVING STANDARD: In 1973 the total labor force in Sweden was about 3.9 million people. The average hourly income for a male industrial worker was $3.77 which means a gross income of 6,480 to 7,680 dollars per year. The average family income is higher, partly due to the fact that a relatively high percentage of married women work outside the home and partly due to family allowances. The national income tax is progressive, while local income tax is a fixed percentage of income. Both taxes are deducted by the employer from each paycheck (the withholding or PAYE system). The Swedish burden of taxation must be said to be heavy when compared to those of other countries. This fact should be considered against the background of existing social services and transfers between income and social benefits.

The following table gives two examples of how many working hours it takes to earn the cost of different items in the family budget. A vacation of four weeks, family allowances, etc., are not taken into consideration.

TABLE II

WORKING HOURS PER YEAR EXPENDED FOR EACH FAMILY BUDGET ITEM, 1973

Income per year	$7,200	$18,000
	Hours	*Hours*
Income taxes & Social Security charges	520	940
Housing, including heat	340	260
Household operation	760	420
Clothing, etc.	180	120
Recreation, health care, transportation, etc.	140	220
Insurance, savings, misc.	60	40
TOTALS	2,000	2,000

At the end of 1972 there were 332 television licenses per 1,000 inhabitants, which means in general that every household had one television set or more. At the same time there were 302 registered passenger cars per 1,000 inhabitants, which also makes about one car per household or more.

SOCIAL INSURANCE: The public old-age pension includes (1) the basic pension and (2) the supplementary pension. The basic pension is generally payable starting the month of one's sixty-seventh birthday. It is financed by governmental income tax. The basic pension is approximately 1,750 dollars annually for single persons and 2,722 dollars for married couples. Since 1960 there has also been a supplementary pension system. The supplementary pension is financed from fees paid by the employer. Self-employed persons pay their own fee. The combined basic and supplementary pensions will equal roughly two-thirds of a pensioner's average income during fifteen best-paid years.

HEALTH INSURANCE: All residents of Sweden are covered by a compulsory health insurance system. A sick person is guaranteed a daily allowance during illness. The aim is to provide about 90 percent of lost income. As of January 1, 1974, either parent at childbirth is eligible for the sickness allowance during a six-month leave of absence from employment or guaranteed six dollars per day if unemployed. On the same date, a national dental insurance system went into effect, whereby 50 percent, or more in some cases, of the treatment cost will be refunded. Health insurance also covers all hospitalization, which in principle is thus free of charge. Visits to doctors at outpatient clinics cost a uniform amount, $2.88. Medicines bought on a doctor's prescription on any one occasion cost a maximum of $3.60, and certain very important medicines such as insulin are free of charge.

OTHER INSURANCE COVERAGE: The industrial injury insurance covers the entire cost of medical and hospital care. It also pays a sickness allowance, as well as death benefits and a survivors' annuity. The employer pays most of the costs for this coverage. Unemployment insurance is the only noncompulsory form of social insurance in Sweden. The great majority of employees have such coverage.

FAMILY AND EDUCATIONAL ALLOWANCES: A child allowance of 360 dollars per year is paid to the parents of each child under sixteen. Children who continue their education are then entitled to a study allowance. Low-income families are also eligible for rent allowances from central and local government, lowering rents considerably.

TAXES: In Sweden the community at large, as represented by departments of the national government (the state) and local government (the municipalities), has assumed responsibility for a great many sectors including education, employment, care of the sick and aged, environment, etc. To discharge its responsibilities the community must lay claim to a fair share of the aggregate resources by means of taxation. Swedish taxes are therefore relatively high, but it must be borne in mind that much of the revenue they yield goes back to the citizens in the form of transfer payments and public services.

The chief source of state revenue is the income tax on individuals and businesses, whereas the local authorities derive most of their revenue from the proportional tax on income. Revenues from indirect taxes, virtually all of which go to the state, are from two main sources: the value added tax and excises on selected commodities.

The state's power to tax is vested in the *Riksdag* (the Swedish Parliament). Local taxes are levied under a system of rules which the *Riksdag* and Cabinet determine in the same way as laws in general. However, the local authorities are free to set the rates of tax in their municipalities. Income tax is paid by individuals earning more than 1,080 dollars per year.

Apart from seamen, who are paid their wages less deductions for income tax, every taxpayer in Sweden is required to file an annual return. Even so, taxes due are largely collected during the year when income is earned: for wage earners under a PAYE (pay as you earn) scheme, and for others by personal prepayment of estimated tax. The authorities then assess each taxpayer's return and send him a bill for his final tax. The difference between this tax and the PAYE or provisional tax determines whether he receives a refund or pays to make up a shortage.

The annual tax on income in varying amounts for a single person is shown in Table III.

TABLE III
DIRECT AND INDIRECT TAXES PAID BY SINGLE PERSONS, 1973

INCOME	$7,200	$18,000	$24,000
Local income tax	$1,423	$ 4,274	$ 5,714
National income tax	623	4,446	7,266
National basic pension charges	296	360	360
Health insurance charges	128	143	143
TOTAL DIRECT TAXES & CHARGES	$2,470	$ 9,223	$13,483
Average indirect taxes			
(value added tax, excises, etc.)	1,182	2,194	2,629
TOTAL TAXES & CHARGES	$3,652	$11,417	$16,112
TOTALS IN PERCENT OF INCOME	51	63	67

LABOR RELATIONS: The Swedish system of industrial relations has long been widely recognized as one of the most stable and harmonious in the world. Very few working days are lost because of disputes, due to the mutual respect and trust between organized labor and management in Sweden. In 1970 the peaceful scene was disrupted by a series of wildcat strikes, but conditions later returned to normal. In the public sector, however, collective bargaining works more smoothly, with only two major conflicts since 1966.

In a European perspective, industrialization in Sweden took place at a relatively late stage. It did not get started until the 1850's and also took a somewhat different turn. While on the Continent and in England industry was located largely in the cities, the pattern in Sweden was to favor small towns.

It follows that unionism was also late in coming to Sweden. Although the first real trade union dates from 1869, the movement did not gather momentum until the 1880's. From then on events moved all the more rapidly, and when LO (the Swedish Confederation of Trade Unions) was established in 1898 unionism acquired the structure it still has today, i.e. with national unions associated in a central organization. The movement ran into strong resistance from the employers, who reacted defensively by setting up "strike insurance societies." Organized management took its present shape in 1902 with the formation of SAF (the Swedish Employers' Confederation).

In spite of management opposition, the determinants of unionism were more favorable in Sweden than in most other countries. The authorities soon adopted a nonintervention policy which left the labor market parties free to regulate their own dealings. One important reason for this was that business interests never carried as much weight in Swedish politics as in most of the great European industrial nations and in the United States. In 1906 the LO and SAF came to an arrangement stipulating that each collective agreement was to contain a clause reading as follows: "Subject to other provisions of this agreement, the employer is entitled to direct and assign the work, to hire and dismiss workers at will, and to employ workers whether they are organized or not." In return the employers promised that the right to organize should be left inviolate.

Despite government nonintervention there arose the need to embody industrial relations in a legal framework, and in 1928 two laws were passed: the Collective Agreements Act and the Labor Court Act. Unions were thus given a means to enforce collective agreements without having to resort to direct action. It is also obvious that the Labor Court soon gained the full confidence of both sides. The Court's composition, with seven members, of whom two are nominated by the employer organizations and two by the unions, has certainly been an important factor, as has its informal procedure.

In the early 1930's the white-collar workers also began to organize, though in unions separate from those of the blue-collar workers. Mainly to protect the new unions a law was passed in 1936: the Act on the Right to Organize and to Bargain Collectively; the blue-collar unions had already reached a stage where they did not need any legal protection. The most important white-collar central organization, TCO (the Swedish Central Organization of Salaried Employees), was founded in 1944. A second central organization in this sector, SACO (the Swedish Confederation of Professional Associations), was formed in 1943. TCO and SACO organize employees both in public and private service. Even though collective bargaining in the public sector has been continuous since the 1940's, civil servants were not granted the right to strike until 1966.

A third organization, SR (the National Federation of Government Officers), is quite small compared to the others, with some 19,000 members. SR primarily organizes commissioned officers in the armed forces and higher ranking officials of the postal service and the railways.

SOCIAL SECURITY: National health insurance provides free medical care at a hospital or clinic. A uniform tariff applies to the public outpatient services. The charges are $2.88 for visiting a doctor at a clinic and $4.80 for a home visit. A tax-free sickness benefit to compensate for loss of income is payable at varying rates according to usual income, amounting to $4.56 a day for a person earning 2,448 to 2,880 dollars a year and $12.48 a day on an income of 9,360 dollars or more a year.

The pension scheme consists of a national basic pension and a supplementary pension. The former is payable to all persons from the age of sixty-seven and in June 1973 amounted to 1,860 dollars a year for a single person and 2,991 dollars for a married couple. If a retired person has only a basic pension and no, or a very low, supplementary pension, he gets about 210 dollars a year in addition to the basic pension. A large number of retired people also receive local housing allowances, tied to the basic pension. These are subject to a means test. In many cases they cover the whole housing cost.

The national supplementary pension is related to previous income and is tied to the cost-of-living index. The benefits payable at any one time will therefore depend on the value of money then prevailing (1957 is the base year). In addition an income ceiling is set, beyond which earnings do not qualify for benefits. The ceiling for 1972 was 11,076 dollars. In July 1972 the supplementary pension came to about $1,920 for a person who earlier earned an income from work of 4,800 dollars and about 6,360 dollars for a person previously earning 12,000 dollars a year. The supplementary pension system is not yet built up completely, and full pension from this system will not be paid until 1981.

The total pension for most persons will amount to about two-thirds of the income earned by the pensioner during his fifteen best-paid years, up to the income ceiling mentioned earlier.

MASS MEDIA

BROADCASTING: All television and radio programs in Sweden are broadcast by Sveriges Radio, a private company operating under a state concession that makes it a virtual monopoly. The Board of Governors consists of eleven members, six appointed by the government including the chairman and five representing the shareholders.

Programming is financed out of license revenues. The current fee for a combined radio and TV license is 53 dollars per year.

General broadcasting policy is laid down by the Radio Act and an Enabling Agreement between Sveriges Radio and the Swedish government. Programs must be impartial and objective and satisfy a broad range of tastes.

From the inception of regular radio broadcasts in 1923 until 1955, Sweden had only one home service. There are now three networks under one program director for sound radio.

Regular telecasts commenced in 1957, when there were 23,000 licenses. In 1972 more than 85 percent of all Swedish homes had

TV sets. Virtually the whole country is capable of receiving at least one of the two channels.

NEWSPAPERS: Under the Freedom of the Press Act, no form of censorship may be applied to Swedish newspapers, magazines, books or brochures. On the other hand, defamation of character, the disclosure of military or other classified secrets, and similar offenses are actionable under criminal law. However, the penalties are always inflicted on the publisher, and the police may not conduct any extralegal inquiries into the sources of an offending article. This protection of anonymity is considered essential to the free exchange of opinions and communication of information. The same purpose is served by the public character of official records, a traditional aspect of Swedish political life that probably has few counterparts elsewhere: Under the terms of legislation which originated 200 years ago, Swedish citizens are guaranteed free access to the official documents of state and local authorities. The liberty to publish such documents is, of course, also extended to the press. Restrictions on this constitutional principle of publicity are recognized only for *privileged communications* (such as medical casebooks) and for military documents.

These provisions of the Freedom of the Press Act embrace all printed material, regardless of scope and frequency of publication.

MOTION PICTURES: Motion pictures intended for public showing in Sweden are viewed beforehand by the National Board of Film Censorship, which is empowered to delete certain sequences or to issue a general ban. Censorship is chiefly exercised on scenes depicting excessive brutality and prurience, on the grounds that these are detrimental to mental health.

GOVERNMENT

Sweden is a constitutional monarchy with a parliamentary form of government. After general elections or the resignation of the cabinet, the leadership of the government goes to the party leader capable of forming a cabinet with the greatest possible support in Parliament. Since 1932, the Social Democratic Labor party has been Sweden's largest party and has been in power, either alone or in coalition with other parties.

A constitutional reform went into effect in 1975, giving the king only symbolic powers. King Gustaf VI Adolf, who ascended the throne in 1950, died in September 1973. He was in turn succeeded by his grandson, King Carl XVI Gustaf.

Parliament consists of one chamber with 350 members who are chosen in direct elections for a three-year term of office. Universal suffrage was introduced in 1921, and the voting age is currently twenty.

At the general election in the autumn of 1973, the various parties received the following share of all votes: Conservatives, 14 percent; Liberal party, 10 percent; Center party, 25 percent; Social Democratic party, 44 percent; Communist party, 5 percent; and others 2 percent. This created a unique political stalemate regarding distribution of parliamentary seats, with 175 going to socialistic parties and 175 to nonsocialistic parties.

It is characteristic of the Swedish constitution that government and administration are two separate functions. The ministries mainly concern themselves with the preparation of new legislative measures to be submitted to Parliament. The execution of legislation and ordinances agreed upon by government and Parliament lies in the hands of central administrative agencies and a regional administrative body in each of the twenty-four counties into which the country is divided. The County Administration is called *länsstyrelse*.

In every county there is also a county council *(landsting)*, which is a popularly elected, parliamentary body. It has the right to impose taxes and is mainly responsible for health and medical care in its geographic area.

THE KING: The Swedish king exerts no political power and takes no part in politics. He represents the nation. According to the Constitution he is Head of State. In this capacity he signs all important decisions of the government. Although formally the king makes the decisions, responsibility for them rests with his "counsellors of state" *(starsråd)*, i.e., the cabinet ministers, who countersign the decisions.

The king opens Parliament *(Riksdag)* in January of each year and addresses it in a short statement. If a cabinet resigns for political reasons it is up to the king to find—on the basis of the strength of the different parties in Parliament—a prime minister who can form a new cabinet with the strongest possible parliamentary support.

The idea of introducing a republican constitution is often openly discussed in the press and at political gatherings. The demand for abolishing the monarchy does not, however, seem to be particularly widespread.

PARLIAMENT: Since 1971, Sweden has had a unicameral Parliament. A constitutional amendment adopted in 1968 and 1969 abolished the bicameral system which had existed since 1866. The whole Parliament is formed by direct election based on a suffrage that comprises all Swedes from the year following that during which they reached nineteen years of age. Parliament has 350 members, who serve three-year terms. Requirements for eligibility are Swedish citizenship and the attainment of voting age. All elections are by proportional representation. The system of elections to Parliament is designed to assure a distribution of seats between the parties in proportion to the votes cast for them nationally. Proportional fairness is not to be primarily achieved in each constituency but in the whole country regarded as a single constituency. Hence, in addition to 310 fixed constituency seats, forty seats are distributed at large to obtain a fair, nationally proportional result. However, the seats at large are also filled by candidates from the parties' regular electoral rolls. There is one exception to the rule on complete national proportionality: a quota rule intended to prevent very small parties from gaining representation in Parliament. A party must thus obtain at least 4 percent of the national popular vote to qualify for representation. In any one constituency, however, a party will gain a seat by obtaining 12 percent of the votes even if its national popular vote falls short of 4 percent.

The trades and professions of Swedish society are fairly well represented in Parliament. No group dominates (the role of school teachers, however, once was conspicuous; lawyers have always been very few). In the present cabinet, every second member has a university education; the corresponding rate among Members of Parliament (MPs) is lower. MPs are often selected among personalities having a strong position in local politics. As a rule they retain such local posts when elected MPs.

The 1809 Instrument of Government was sustained by the idea of a separation of powers between king and Parliament. But for the work of constitutional reform that has been going on ever since the 1950's, the cardinal task instead is to have a written constitution embody the present actual polity based on democracy and parliamentarianism. Since this policy builds upon the principle of popular sovereignity, the Parliament elected by the people occupies the leading position and is fundamentally the preeminent organ of state. Parliament is the foundation for the democratic exercise of power through the government.

THE CABINET: Political power rests with the cabinet *(regering)* and the party or parties it represents. There are at present nineteen ministers in the Social Democratic Cabinet. The prime minister *(statsminister)* has at his side twelve heads of ministry. They are the ministers of (1) justice, (2) foreign affairs, (3) defense, (4) health and social affairs, (5) communications, (6) finance, (7) education and cultural affairs, (8) agriculture, (9) commerce, (10) labor and housing, (11) physical planning and local government, and (12) industry. The present cabinet also includes six ministers without portfolio. One of these is in charge of *family policy;* another is a consultant in foreign affairs. Two are legal consultants, one deals with educational matters and one with civil service affairs.

The prime minister selects the cabinet members, whose nominations, like his own, are not subject to any formal approval by Parliament. Nominations are formally decided by the king. So are dismissals, but here the Instrument of Government explicitly states how the king must decide. In the case of a minister, his dismissal must be based on a vote of censure taken by Parliament unless new elections are ordered; otherwise, dismissals take place if the prime minister so requests. See the following chart of the Ministry of Justice.

SWEDISH MINISTRY OF JUSTICE *(Justitiedepartementet)*

	Staff	Primary function
National Police Board *(Rikspolisstyrelsen)*	460	Central authority for the police administration which has a total personnel of approximately 17,100
Chief Public Prosecutor *(Riksåklagaren)*	40	Head of the public prosecution authorities which have a total personnel of approximately 1,139
National Corrections Administration *(Kriminalvårdsstyrelsen)*	235	Central authority for the correctional administration which has a total personnel of approximately 4,000

FUNCTIONS OF MINISTRIES: The ministries *(departements)* are small units, each as a rule consisting of no more than 100 persons (including clerical staff). They are concerned with (1) preparing the government's bills (propositions) to Parliament on budget appropriations and laws, (2) issuing laws and regulations and general rules for the administrative agencies, (3) international relations, (4) higher appointments in the administration, and (5) certain appeals from individuals, which according to historical patterns are addressed to the king. Except for appeals, the ministries are in most fields not concerned with details of administration. Matters concerning the practical implementation of legislation or general rules may, however, in different ways, i.e. through the mass media, be brought before the ministries.

WORKING METHODS OF THE CABINET: The cabinet as a whole is responsible for all government decisions. Although in practice a great number of routine matters are decided upon by individual ministers and only formally confirmed by the government, the principle of collective responsibility is reflected in all forms of governmental work.

Once a week the formal decisions of the government are made, hundreds of them in half an hour or so, at a meeting in the Royal Palace presided over by the king and attended by the ministers (the king in council). The practice is that before these meetings the king is informed of decisions which are of major importance or in which the ministers know he takes a personal interest.

All important decisions to be made by the government are subject to discussion by the cabinet as a whole. Plenary cabinet meetings under the chairmanship of the prime minister are normally held one to three times a week. At these meetings top officials often introduce the matters at hand and reply to questions raised by ministers, whereupon the cabinet discussion and decision proceed behind closed doors. No minutes are taken.

As a rule cabinet members lunch together in their private restaurant in the chancery building, where no other guests are admitted. In practice, a great number of decisions are made quite informally at these luncheons after a briefing given by the minister concerned.

A third, even less formal kind of cabinet decision-making is that of two or three ministers concerned discussing a matter, with or without the presence of subordinate officials from their ministries, in order to reach agreement without taking up the time of the cabinet as a whole.

The working method thus described allows for a high degree of coordination between all the branches of government in matters of policy. The officials of the ministries meet often and easily with each other and prepare decisions. Before becoming final and public, all decisions of interest to more than one ministry are commented upon by top officials of the ministries concerned. An important feature of the working methods of the government is that all government bills to be presented and important pronouncements (answers to questions, etc.) by individual ministers to be made in Parliament on behalf of the government are circulated beforehand to all ministers for their written comments. This system allows for information to, and discussion between, cabinet ministers and top officials before the formal decisions are made. It also gives the legal consultants of cabinet rank an opportunity to function as legal supervisors and coordinators of all government actions.

The highest-ranking officials of the ministry are the under-secretary of state *(statssekreterare)*, the permanent secretary *(expeditionchef)*, and the chief legal officer *(rättschef)*.

The under secretary of state is responsible to the minister for leading the work within the ministry. It is thus up to him to plan the ministry's work, to supervise the carrying out of this work, and to establish the necessary coordination between the activities of the different ministerial units.

The permanent secretary supervises the legality and consistency of administrative decisions to be made within the ministry and is responsible for the final drafting of government decisions to be dispatched from the ministry.

The chief legal officer is mainly responsible for the drafting of laws and regulations within the ministry's sphere of authority.

The under secretaries of state—one in each ministry—are, generally speaking, the only political appointees of the ministries. Yet a number of them are not known as party affiliates, i.e., they do not take part in the political debate. Many of them are rather known as nonpolitical officials. Occasionally an under secretary is a member of Parliament. An under secretary who is not an MP is not entitled to speak in Parliament, but there is a listener's seat for him in the assembly hall. Whether an affiliate to his minister's party or not, the under secretary represents the ministry and the minister. He is often a delegate to international conferences.

All officials of the ministries are appointed by the government, Parliament having no right to intervene or pass judgment on the appointments.

In case of a change of party in office, very few changes in the cadre of officials are likely to occur. A few undersecretaries of state would resign. Some political experts who are employed by the ministries for nonfixed terms would leave.

On the other hand, all civil servants in Sweden, and military and police personnel as well, are perfectly free to take part in political life and to hold political office.

ADMINISTRATIVE ORGANIZATION: The carrying out of government decisions is entrusted to a number of central administrative agencies.

Every such agency is headed by a director general, appointed by the government, as a rule for a period of six years at a time. The board of an agency consists of the director general as chairman and a number of senior officials serving next under him and some laymen, representing organizations or sections of the population having special interest in the matters dealt with by the agency concerned. In many cases membership of the board is confined to the director general and a number of laymen. All these members of the boards are appointed by the government, as are senior officials of the agencies. Personnel of lower grades are appointed by the board itself.

The administrative agencies are under obligation to cooperate with each other directly, without the interference of ministerial bodies.

TENURE OF CIVIL SERVANTS: The security of tenure, which almost all civil servants enjoy, is an important feature. They are appointed for their lifetime and can be removed before their retirement age only as a result of legal procedure due to breach of duty or criminal offense. This means that a civil servant can be held legally responsible before a court of law rather than before his superior for the way he carries out his duties.

Even top officials, appointed for a limited period or until further notice, are seldom or never removed from their posts other than by agreement between the parties concerned.

THE PRINCIPLE OF PUBLICITY: Official documents are, to a great extent, accessible to the press and to private citizens. All files of any administrative office are open to the public if not declared secret for reasons related to military security, international relations, or the personal interest of individuals concerned (because they contain criminal or medical records and the like). Nobody has to show cause for seeing a public document. On the other hand, during the preparation of a decision, working material cannot be requested for public use.

THE ATTORNEY GENERAL: The Instrument of Government also provides for the office of attorney general *(justitiekansler)*, who supervises the courts and administrative organs with particular concern for safeguarding the interests of the Crown. The attorney general, who is a cabinet appointee and usually a man with a distinguished record of service in the judiciary, follows the same procedures as the ombudsman. Thus, he makes frequent trips to inspect official records and documents in detail. He also has authority to represent the Crown in civil litigation and serves the cabinet as its chief legal advisor.

POLITICAL PARTIES: The five parties in Parliament are the Social Democratic Labor Party *(Social-demokratiska Arbetarepartiet),* the Liberal Party *(Folkpartiet* or the People's Party), the Conservative Party *(Moderata Samlingspartiet),* the Center Party *(Centerpartiet,* formerly the Farmers' Party), and the Communist Party *(Vänsterpartiet Kommunisterna).*

The parties are well organized both in Parliament and outside. The Social Democratic Party is closely allied with the workers' trade union movement *(Landsorganisationen* or LO), which has a number of representatives in Parliament as Social Democrats.

Beginning in 1966, state subsidies have been paid to every political party represented in Parliament which is regularly engaged in opinion-molding activities. To qualify for the subsidy, each party must have won at least one seat in the most recent general election and acquired at least 2 percent of the national popular vote.

Since 1932 the Social Democrats have been in office permanently, except for a period of 100 days in 1936. Between 1933 and 1936 they had a working agreement with the Center Party. Coalition governments of Social Democrats and the Center were in power from 1936 to 1939 and 1951 to 1957. During the Second World War, 1939 to 1945, all parties except the Communists were in coalition. During the years 1945 to 1951 and since 1957, the Social Democrats have been in office alone.

Since 1942 the Social Democrats alone have had the majority of votes in the First Chamber. For a long time they have commanded a majority of more votes than the three nonsocialist parties combined. In the new unicameral Parliament, reflecting the outcome of the 1970 election, the Social Democratic cabinet lacks an absolute majority. Together the nongoverning parties have more seats than the Social Democrats. The government thus depends on support from one of these parties in order to gain a majority for its proposals.

All political organizations enjoy full freedom and all democratic rights.

THE ROLE OF ORGANIZATIONS: Representatives of organizations of different kinds sit in Parliament, serve on commissions of inquiry, and belong to administrative agencies. The organizations are invited to submit comments on all sorts of proposals within the administration of Parliament. Their views are recorded in the official publications of the political machinery.

The above applies to the organizations of trade unions, salaried employees, employers, consumers' and producers' cooperatives, smallholders, industry, business, trade, women, tenants, landlords, etc.

It would seem that *pressure groups* in Sweden should not really be called by that name. The organizations form regular parts of the democratic system itself. Not only are they involved in public discussion, they also play a responsible part in actual administration at all levels. (They also serve on many regional or local administrative bodies.)

It is probably fair to say that, by the methods described, the organizations exert a considerable influence in Swedish political life.

LOCAL ADMINISTRATION: Before 1971 Sweden was divided into 850 municipalities *(kommun)*, each with an elected assembly. This number has been reduced since 1974 to 270 municipalities. The powers and duties of the municipalities relate to the provision of a great number of necessities and facilities: housing and supplements thereto, such as roads, sewerage and water supply, basic education, public assistance, and child welfare.

They have the right to levy income taxes and receive the revenue from a modest tax on real estate.

Between the state and the municipality, there is a regional organization composed of twenty-four counties. The national administration in each of these counties is represented by a governor *(landshövding)* and the county administration *(länsstyrelse)*. The governors are appointed by the government for six-year terms; they are often chosen from among politicians but normally leave the political scene upon their appointment.

For certain tasks of a fundamentally municipal character, the municipalities of each county are united in a county council *(landsting)*, for which the same rules apply as in other elected local or national bodies. These assemblies are responsible primarily for health services and certain types of education and vocational training. The county councils are entitled to impose an income tax to cover their expenses.

OMBUDSMAN

Protecting the rights of the citizen in his encounters with administrative authority is fundamental to due process of law in Sweden. The task of reviewing the acts of government officials and administrators is entrusted to the Parliamentary ombudsban (JO).

However, Sweden has other ombudsmen, too. One is the antitrust ombudsman (NO), who looks after compliance with the Restrictive Trade Practices Act. Another is the consumer ombudsman (KO), whose job is to enforce two laws: the Marketing Practices Act and the Act Prohibiting Improper Contract Terms.

Then there is the press ombudsman (PO), who among other things investigates charges of libel or inaccurate publicity with the aim of ensuring that these do not necessarily reach the point of litigation in court.

THE PARLIAMENTARY OMBUDSMAN (JO): This office dates back to 1809 and was originally established to provide the Parliament (Riksdag) with a means of controlling the observance of laws and ordinances by all judges, civil servants, and military officers.

When the burden of work became too much for the JO to handle, the *Riksdag* voted to establish another office to look after military affairs exclusively. This new parliamentary commissioner, the military ombudsman (MO), was appointed in 1915.

The cleavage lasted until "1968" when both officers were merged anew and three ombudsmen of equal status, all called JO, were appointed.

Although the ombudsmen formally serve a four-year term, extensions are customarily granted. Should any one of them commit a serious breach of duty, the *Riksdag* may dismiss him, but that has not happened yet. By declining to reappoint him (and this has happened), the *Riksdag* can indicate that an ombudsman does not enjoy the confidence of the *Riksdag*.

As part of the reorganization in 1968, separate jurisdictions were defined for the three ombudsmen.

INSPECTIONS: Back in the nineteenth century an ombudsman spent much of his time on the road, but when his case load became too heavy in the early twentieth century, the number of inspection trips had to be cut down. Under the new dispensation, however, the JO is again more active in the field. He makes regular inspections of courts, army posts, prisons, etc. Inspecting local representatives of the king in council such as county government boards also comes within his purview.

The JO's control of administrative agencies might be called "roving inspections." The agency involved is notified some days ahead. On assignments of this kind, the JO takes assistants with him to examine the agency's reports. If a case of maladministration is suspected, the person responsible is first given opportunity to be heard. Two alternatives are available to the JO in his capacity of prosecutor: Usually, he will initiate a written inquiry, but if the case is more serious he may also hold oral hearings with the respondent.

INVESTIGATIONS: The JO also pursues investigations on a long-term basis. These often entail reviews of laws and their enforcement. Suggestions for this form of control come to the JO from various sources: often people who complain or articles in a magazine or newspaper. The JO need not show cause for undertaking an investigation.

COMPLAINTS FROM THE PUBLIC: Any citizen who feels he has been wronged may submit a written complaint to the JO. In 1972, 3,187 such complaints were handled. Around 1,200 cases were concerned with the criminal justice system, of which the largest number of complaints (365) pertained to prison administration, followed by medical care (331), police (272), courts (259), and taxation and revenues (199). JO is unable to deal with all cases but must concentrate on those which have importance in terms of striking a just balance between the claims of the community and the freedom of the individual. Many of the complaints come from people who have gotten caught in a bureaucratic merry-go-round.

The *Riksdag* has empowered the JO with full discretion to decide which cases should be investigated. Many cases are referred to agencies who command better expertise than the JO, such as the National Board of Health and Welfare and the National Correctional Administration.

SUPERVISION: The Parliamentary ombudsmen's office enjoys full autonomy in relation to its principal, the *Riksdag*, which does not have the right to issue directives. On the other hand, the JO's official report is examined by one of the standing parliamentary committees. After examining the contents on a spot-check basis, the committee presents a statement of opinion to the *Riksdag,* whose members may then debate what the JO should and should not have done in different cases.

The mass media may also be said to function as bodies of control over the JO, since they often take up controversial cases for debate.

THE ANTITRUST OMBUDSMAN (NO): Unlike the JO, the antitrust ombudsman (NO) is appointed not by the *Riksdag* but by the king in council. The NO's office was set up in 1954 and now has a staff of about twenty persons.

The NO's activities are based on the Restrictive Trade Practices Act, which is the name of the Swedish antitrust law. The purpose of this law is to promote such competition in the economy as is desirable in the public interest. Two types of restrictive trade practices are prohibited under sanction of criminal penalties: resale price maintenance and collusive tendering. But exemptions may be granted under certain conditions.

Otherwise, Swedish antitrust law is not based on rigid rules backed by criminal sanctions. Instead, it has devised what may be termed the method of negotiations for eliminating harmful effects of restraints of competition. There are three essential elements of this method: (1) general and specific fact-finding based on far-reaching powers under the Investigation Act, (2) publicity, and (3) informal negotiations aimed at preventing or eliminating undesirable practices. A restraint of competiton shall be deemed to have harmful effects if, contrary to the public interest, it unduly affects the formation of prices, restrains productivity in business, or prevents the trade of others.

THE CONSUMER OMBUDSMAN (KO): Like the NO, the consumer ombudsman is appointed by the king in council. He took office on January 1, 1971, with the duty of ensuring that two laws for the protection of consumers are observed: the Marketing Practices Act and the Act Prohibiting Improper Contract Terms.

The aim of the Marketing Practices Act is to protect consumers against misleading advertising and other undesirable commercial marketing. By the provisions of the general clause of the Act, any marketing activity deemed to be undesirable from the viewpoint of consumers or entrepreneurs can be prohibited. The act also explicitly prohibits intentionally misleading advertising, some kinds of discount stamps which are obtained if a commodity or service is bought, and certain combined offers of goods. The KO checks that advertising contains no misleading information about products, prices, quality, etc.; supervises all kinds of commercial marketing carried out by private or public entrepreneurs; and scrutinizes advertising in newspapers and periodicals, on packages, and direct-mail advertising, etc.

THE PRESS OMBUDSMAN (PO): The Swedish Press Council or Court of Honor, founded in 1916, is probably the oldest tribunal of its kind in the world. It was formed by the National Press Club (PK), the Union of Journalists (SJF), and the Newspaper Publishers Association (TU).

The court is composed of a jurist, who acts as chairman; one representative each from PK, SJF, and TU; plus two representatives of the public who must not have any ties with newspaper publishers or press organizations.

The office of press ombudsman was established on November 1, 1969. Its holder is appointed by a special committee of three persons, including the parliamentary ombudsman, the chairman of the Swedish Bar Association, and the chairman of the Press Cooperation Board. Thus, the press has deliberately abstained from exercising a majority in the choice of press ombudsman.

FOREIGN POLICY AND INTERNATIONAL COOPERATION

The aim of Sweden's foreign policy is nonalignment in peacetime and neutrality in wartime. The country has not fought a war since 1814. Sweden has been a member of the United Nations since 1946 and has played an active role there, for example in disarmament talks and in providing mediators, observers, and troops for UN peacekeeping operations.

Sweden is a member of practically all the UN special agencies and of the Council of Europe. Together with Denmark, Finland, Iceland, and Norway, Sweden belongs to the Nordic Council, a joint parliamentary advisory body. The five countries have a common labor market, extensive coordination of social welfare legislation, and a passport union. For the time being, Sweden has chosen to sign only a free trade agreement with the European communities, since Sweden's policy of neutrality and nonalignment is felt to exclude the possibilities of either full membership or association.

NATIONAL DEFENSE: Sweden's nonaligned foreign policy is regarded as making a strong defense system necessary. Military service is compulsory for all men between eighteen and forty-seven years of age and consists of a basic period of training that lasts seven and a half to fifteen months. The defense budget amounts to about 4 percent of Sweden's gross national product.

LAW

Swedish law as it exists today is the result of a long historical development marked by continuity rather than abrupt changes. The most important source of constitutional law is still the Instrument of Government dating from 1809. In a number of important areas, substantial changes have been made. Since 1954 a general review of the fundamental laws has been in progress, and on the basis of this a partial constitutional reform was carried out in 1969. A proposal for a completely new constitution was put forward in 1973.

The Act of Succession (on the present Royal Family) dates to 1866. These acts have been revised by a commission, and Parliament has resolved in favor of the introduction of the unicameral system of representation. By virtue of the same reform decision in 1968 and 1969, parliamentary rule (or at least certain aspects of it) has also been codified in the Instrument of Government. The fourth constitutional act, the Freedom of the Press Act, in its present shape is dated 1949.

The Swedish system of government as it has been developed until the present day may be described as a representative monarchy with democracy. This means that at elections held at regular intervals with universal suffrage and with equality of voting rights, the citizens elect a decision-making assembly, the *Riksdag* (the Swedish Parliament). Another cornerstone of the Swedish system of government is parliamentarianism. The most recent development in this area means that the government's dependence on the *Riksdag* has been still further affirmed. Since the first few decades of the present century, the king has been without political power. Formerly, however, his authority was considerable.

As far as civil law and criminal law are concerned, the National Law Code of 1734 is still in force, at least officially. However, little of the Code's original contents remains. The majority of the *balkar* or books into which the National Law Code of 1734 is divided have, however, been replaced during the present century. Thus, there have come into existence completely new books for marriage, wills and successions, real property, criminal offences, and judicial procedure. In modern times, moreover, a mass of special legislation has grown outside the Code in such fields as company law, copyright, protection of industrial property, and labor relations. In the case of public law, too, important legislation has been passed in recent times, not least in the fields of town and country planning, environmental protection, and nature conservation.

GENERAL CHARACTERISTICS OF LAW: Swedish legislation is based on a strong domestic tradition of Germanic law, but it has also been influenced by foreign law. Roman law has had less influence on developments than in most of the European countries. In a number of areas, however, influences from Roman law can be traced, while in other areas there can be clearly observed features drawn from German, French, and in later times, Anglo-American law. An important difference in relation to the majority of Continental legal systems is that Sweden has abstained from large-scale codifications along the lines of the *Code Civil* in France or the *Bürgerliches Gesetzbuch* in Germany. In comparison with Anglo-American law, a major difference in Swedish law is that it is based to a considerably greater extent on written law while judicial practice plays a smaller, though important role. Thus, the Swedish legal system, both by virtue of its systematic structure and its contents, may be said to be at a point half way between the Continental European and Anglo-American systems.

LAWMAKING TODAY: A brisk pace of legislation has been maintained in Sweden for the past few decades. As mentioned earlier, several important sectors have been overhauled in their entirety. An important characteristic of Swedish lawmaking is that, since the end of the nineteenth century, so much of it is being prepared in collaboration with the other Nordic countries. The result has been to achieve a significant degree of legal uniformity in Scandinavia, especially in the field of civil law.

Sweden has been ruled for forty years by a Social Democratic government, whose statements of policy have committed it, at least in principle, to sweeping social changes. At the same time, however, the Social Democrats have always had to contend with a powerful nonsocialist opposition. The ruling party's objectives have found expression in the statute books, particularly as regards taxation, social welfare, and those areas which have relevance in terms of national planning. On the other hand, the political infighting has so far had little effect on criminal and civil law. Lately, however, in a number of areas of civil legislation, the conception of the community's interests deriving from the politically dominant philosophy has brought about modifications in the traditional principles regarding private ownership and freedom of contract.

The powers that we have also treaded warily in regard to constitutional and parliamentary procedures, as well as in matters relating to the organization of administration and justice. It is still true to say that Swedish public life is permeated to an unusually high degree by the ideals of a law-governed society. While this holds for the courts as a matter of course, it is noteworthy that the administrative authorities should also embrace judiciary forms to such a great extent for their own work; while it is not, or at least was not, uncommon in other Western European states for administrators to claim the discretionary powers of a private businessman, their Swedish counterparts have long followed the dictates of written law or well-established precedents.

It can be asserted, by way of summing up, that Swedish law in its broad organic aspect exhibits a rather peculiar mixture of traditionalism and radicalism. This helps explain the decided penchant for compromises and middle-of-the-road solutions that have characterized the political climate.

THE LAWMAKING PROCESS: The preparation of bills is done by commissions of inquiry, legal experts in the ministries, and *Riksdag* committees. Initiatives for new legislation can come from the government or a government agency, from professional organizations and trade unions, or from other associations. Another common procedure is that whereby the *Riksdag,* on the basis of motions introduced by individual members, makes representations for an inquiry to be made concerning the legislation on a certain question. It is nowadays the exception rather than the rule for one or more members of the *Riksdag* to present a complete legal draft for consideration.

COMMISSIONS OF INQUIRY: As a first step the sponsoring minister, with the approval of the king in council, appoints a commission of inquiry. If the proposed measure has political implications, the commission will usually consist of politicians from different parties and representatives of important interest groups, presided over by a high-ranking judge or civil servant. Junior judges will usually officiate as experts and secretaries.

When a commission has finished its work, its recommendations are examined by the affected ministry's legislative department. The commission's report is then sent out for submissions, i.e. for comment by interested authorities and organizations.

The most important part of the *Riksdag's* legislative work is performed within committees which are organized according to subject areas mainly following the ministerial division. Their composition reflects the political division of strength in the *Riksdag.* Every committee has access to experts within its field.

If the *Riksdag* approves the cabinet's bill as proposed, the king in council promulgates a law in accordance therewith. If the *Riksdag* makes amendments, the bill may be referred again to the Law Council for a statement of opinion, after which the cabinet is required to decide upon the *Riksdag* proposals.

CHAPTER 4

THE POLICE ORGANIZATION

H ISTORY: In order to understand law enforcement as a contemporary phenomena of social interaction, it will be of interest to briefly trace the evolution of this human institution in its task of maintaining domestic peace and order.

Police development tends to move from simple to complex structures producing a manifestation of change. Francis Bacon (1561-1626) once stated, "He who will not apply new remedies must expect new evils, for time is the greatest innovator." As the enforcer of criminal and regulatory law, police have been the institution primarily concerned with the control of disruptive deviant behavior.

In Sweden the urban watch and ward and the rural bailiffs were similar to those institutions found elsewhere in northern and western Europe since the early Medieval Age. While the impact of Continental administrative philosophy and law was impressive, a classification of the legal tradition would probably place the Nordic countries between the Roman Law and the Common Law systems.

From the Age of Enlightenment the German administrative concepts and procedures were imitated. However, Sweden did not coordinate policing at the central level until the twentieth century (1965). The modern organization of local Swedish government since 1862 adheres to similar municipal reforms initiated in Germany and England.

A disciplined environment facilitates social control. The Swedes seem to rely on individual compliant performance at a higher level than what is found in Anglo-American communities. The bureaucracy places great emphasis on regulation which in turn becomes an effective means for community adaptability. It is significant that the collegiate boards are responsible for keeping informed about the work in related fields in other countries.[1] By paying this attention to comparative (international) analyses, probably the trial and error period is reduced. It appears that public control efforts to cope with man's ever expanding application of knowledge must change to meet new technology and information.

The early Enlightenment regarded the concept of police as a general government function with specific reference to the regulation of human interaction. Gradually, the tasks of domestic order, the protection of life and property, and the control of crime were delegated to a body headed by a city police chief. This facilitated some separation between politics and police. In 1776 Stockholm was organized in this way, and soon other towns followed.

Police regulations portrayed the impact of the French prototype of 1667 with a lieutenant general of police. The transition from the watch and ward to an organization of constables in the middle of the nineteenth century was a partial imitation of Robert Peel's reforms in England and the establishment of the Metropolitan Police of London in 1829. Structurally, however, the Nordic police continued to conform to the continental European practice in the variety of tasks assigned to them.

During the nineteenth century Sweden had approximately 600 independent police forces with 70 percent of them having less than ten police officers. This system proved inadequate in policing a mobile complex society.

Pursuant to several public studies the Parliament in 1925 passed a bill which anticipated a national police establishment. It also created municipal advisory citizens' boards.

The violence that accompanied the industrial unrest of the 1930's domestic and worldwide economic depression compelled the central governments in all Nordic countries to establish state police forces to reinforce local police. Since 1932 units of the state police were strategically placed throughout Sweden to assist local police. In 1936 the county commissioner's powers relative to the municipal police forces were strengthened, though the county administrative board remained the highest authority.

At the conclusion of many studies by governmental commissions, Parliament in 1962 voted in principle to nationalize the police. The reform was implemented in 1965 by the appointment of a director general with a working staff. The amalgamation of police districts reduced the number to 119 local police departments, centrally financed and coordinated. Refer to Figure 1 for a description of the police districts. The local advisory police boards some years later were replaced by decision-making boards. Operational independence rested with the local police chiefs who could draw on national resources when faced with complicated problems.

The police organization has a regional overlay of eight jurisdictions to coordinate policing and inspection in matters not requiring the attention of the National Police Board. The tasks that are appropriate for regional coordination would include the following: (1) traffic supervision, (2) surveillance and reporting on special crimes, (3) reinforcement of local police, (4) reallocation of equipment, and (5) personnel information and investigation pertaining to recruitment. In the metropolitan areas of Stockholm, Gothenburg, and Malmö, the city police chiefs have assumed the regional responsibilities. The remaining five regions have county police commissioners as chiefs. Thus, a flexible system has been created which allows for personnel to be deployed according to the demands of service. This consideration has taken into account mobile crime as well as the need for increased police supervision of road traffic to reduce accidents.

In line with the practice throughout Europe since feudal times, the local police chief combines in his office peacekeeping functions, judicial authority, jail administration, and bailiff's duties. Practical considerations also conform to important democratic principles resulting in a separation of regular police functions from prosecution and the bailiff.

In addition to the director general or chief police commissioner, there are also the deputy commissioner and six members of the ruling board representing the major political parties in Parliament. The national police is in Stockholm and comprises a secretariat, four departments, nine bureaus, a computer unit, the police school and the police academy, two training units, and the national criminal investigation department. This functional organization distinguishes between the tasks of preserving order by visible, uniformed police surveillance, the regulation of road traffic, the control of crime, and repression of subversive activity.

It should be noted that there are no separate, special police

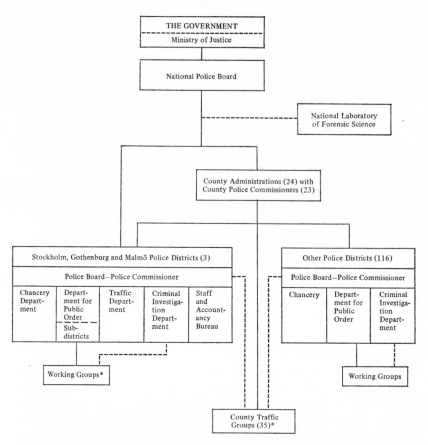

Figure 1. The Swedish police system, 1973. *Not in Stockholm Police District.

agencies in Sweden similar to United States federal law enforcement organizations but rather a unitary and comprehensive police department with duties that in the United States have been assigned to the Immigration and Naturalization Service, the Secret Service, Postal Inspection, Drug Enforcement Administration, etc., to mention only a few complexities of a huge federal system.

Another significant feature has been the functional separation between the police executive operations and the scientific analysis of crime evidence. The National Laboratory of Forensic Science (SKL) is an academic research institute whose director is a professor with a Ph.D. This makes the presentation of evidence in the law courts less likely to be challenged by defense attorneys. The institute is linked administratively to the National Police Board (RPS).

POLICE ORGANIZATION

The National Police Board in 1973 published an official description of the structural-functional framework. This will be adhered to in the following explanation in order to clarify the workings of the Swedish police. See Figure 2 for a graphic presentation of the National Swedish Police Board (NSPB).

Secretariat

This position facilitates the coordination, follow-up, and planning for which the director general and his deputy are responsible. It embraces the information unit for internal and external matters, the Police Museum, and the library. The information unit supervises the issuance of the publications *Swedish Police (Svensk Polis)* and the *General Bulletins (Allmänna Meddelanden)*. Furthermore, it publishes press releases and public information. The unit distributes crime prevention leaflets jointly with the other board units and assists in arranging mobile police exhibitions at the regional and local levels. It assumes a major responsibility for the annual Police Day and events of a social nature to promote public support. Additional responsibilities include public relations, internal information, and military liaison.

Operations Department

The Operations Department has two divisions:

DIVISION I: This division deals primarily with the uniformed branch responsible for public order and traffic. Its field of work covers mainly the preservation of law and order and the supervision and regulation of road traffic. This division also includes a surveillance section that prepares standards, methods, and instructions for surveillance work and estimates the need for policemen, cars, dogs, etc. Plans for procedure in the event of alerts and emergency situations, mountain rescue, search and rescue (SAR) work,

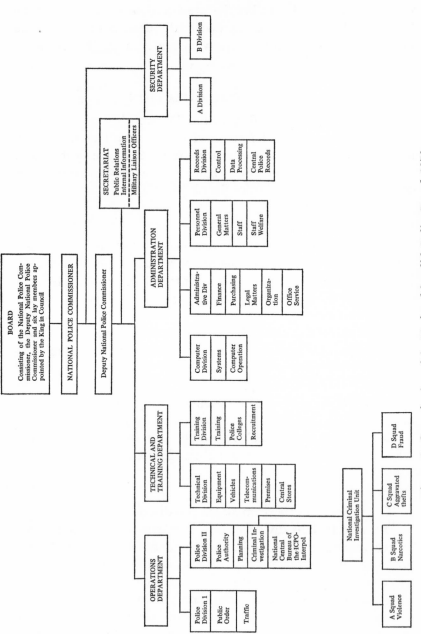

Figure 2. Organization of the National Swedish Police Board, 1973.

and the sea police are also part of the duties of this bureau. Moreover, this section is responsible for the allocation of personnel to police districts for surveillance work and for their employment.

The traffic section plans and coordinates traffic surveillance and nationwide activities requiring helicopter operations. Matters concerning assignment of personnel for traffic duties as well as deployment are handled by this section. In addition, it issues instructions for road safety education in schools and maintains contact with authorities and organizations concerned with traffic safety, i.e. the National Road Safety Office (TSV) and the National Swedish Road Safety Organization (NTF).

DIVISION II: This division could also be called the criminal division, although it deals partly with matters other than criminal investigations. The most important duties are detection and investigative work and operational command of investigations carried out on a national basis.

1. *Police Authority:* This section is responsible for coordinating police authorities and traffic committees and giving information to the government on constitutional questions relating to practices and procedures for investigations and police activities. This section also issues the publication *Rättsnytt* (judicial news). It also gives instructions, advice, and recommendations on matters concerning aliens.

2. *Planning:* This section handles matters concerning planning and rationalization with regard to investigative work; the local records; preliminary investigations; and coordination between the police, the prosecution authority, and the courts. The section also deals with matters concerning police and traffic accident statistics and working statistics for investigations in police districts. Moreover, this section is responsible for estimating the allocation of personnel to the police district for investigative work.

3. *Criminal Investigation* coordinates detection and investigative work dealing with crime on a national level. The section directs activity in the National Criminal Investigation Department (NCID) which consists of about 100 qualified detectives specializing in particular crimes. They are organ-

ized into four squads: violence, narcotics, thefts and fraud.

The criminal section is also concerned with planning and research of working methods and routines and the issuing of instructions for protection, detection, and crime prevention. In these activities the section cooperates with other authorities and organizations involved. In addition, the National Criminal Investigation Department serves as a reinforcement to the local police when investigating crimes requiring specialized knowledge or a particularly large number of people.

4. *The National Central Bureau* carries out the duties incumbent upon the National Swedish Police Board within the International Criminal Police Organization (Interpol). The duty of the section is to maintain contact with the General Secretariat in Paris and the national bureaus of other countries. Thus, the section functions as a service organization for authorities concerned with the maintenance of law and order in Sweden, in their contact with corresponding organizations in other countries. Major responsibilities deal with international search for wanted persons, extraditions, interrogations or other criminal investigations, and investigations of a general nature affecting international police work.

Technical and Training Department

TECHNICAL DIVISION: The demand for technical improvement of the police system has been emphasized during recent years. In order to satisfy this demand the Technical Division was created when the police were reorganized. The division consists of the following five sections:

1. *Equipment:* This section is responsible for acquiring equipment for vehicles, traffic surveillance, mountain rescue, crime investigation, and horses and dogs. It is also responsible for issuing directions on the use and care of equipment.

2. *Vehicles:* The vehicle section is responsible for the acquisition and maintenance of all vehicle equipment which includes not only cars and motorcycles, but also boats, heli-

copters, and snow scooters. It also handles technical matters concerning air ambulances and rescue aircraft (SAR aircraft).

3. *Telecommunications* is responsible for radio and telecommunications. A modernization program of the police radio network started in 1970, and since the beginning of 1973 a more efficient radio system (System 70) has been in use in the whole country. A special radio network has also been set up in mountain areas.

4. The Buildings section deals with police premises in cooperation with the National Board of Public Building. Its duties include planning in connection with the building of new premises, and additional work or rebuilding of existing premises for the police.

5. *Central Stores* assumes the quartermaster function of all other equipment and supplies.

TRAINING DIVISION: The comprehensive training activity of the police is planned, administered, and to a great extent carried out by the training division.

The main part of the planning is carried out by the training section which in cooperation with other divisions within the National Swedish Police Board works out the contents of the different courses and the annual training assignments for police colleges, counties, and police districts. The section is also responsible for coordination and educational development of police training.

A recruitment section is also part of the training division, being the central unit for recruiting personnel for the police chief and police officer arm of the force.

Having been admitted to training, policemen obtain their basic training at the Police College in Ulriksdal, where certain central courses are held as well. The training for those admitted to police chief training, like all other officers' training courses, takes place at the Police College in Solna. Centrally arranged training in motor vehicle duties and traffic surveillance takes place at the police section of the Swedish Army Driving School in Strängnäs, and training of dog handlers at the police section of the Swedish Armed Forces' Dog Training Center in Solleftea. Moreover, certain special training, i.e. mountain training, water rescue, etc., is located in other places in the country, chosen because of their geographic location and availability.

Altogether central training includes about 150 different courses per year. The basic training and the officers' training courses at the police colleges in Ulriksdal and Solna include instruction in general police theory, criminal law, civil law, Swedish, English, psychology, medicine, knowledge of motor vehicles, and physical training.

In addition to the basic police course which lasts approximately forty weeks, there are the following training programs: (1) A higher police course is to be taken three to five years after completion of the basic course. Emphasis in this training is on general police knowledge, and the course is compulsory for all police officers. (2) The sergeant's course is taken after promotion to sergeant. In addition to extending his knowledge, the course is intended to exercise the student's capacity for coping independently with various tasks associated with police duties. (3) A lieutenant's course deals with administrative functions, i.e. management techniques and their practical application and police organization. (4) A captain's course is designed to provide a knowledge of police tactics, management, organization of work and staff, fiscal management, and legal characteristics. (5) The precinct commander's course provides instruction for the organization and direction of police work within a police district, management at the executive level, planning and control, and personnel administration.

Training which for practical reasons cannot be carried out centrally is instead taken care of regionally through the respective county police commissioners, or locally as the responsibility of the police commissioner of the police district in question. Local training includes primarily physical training and use of weapons.

Administration Department

COMPUTER DIVISION: This unit is divided into a systems section and an operations section. The Computer Division is also responsible for the development, operation, and maintenance of automated data processing (ADP) systems.

The number of systems in production has increased rapidly,

totaling about forty. These systems consist both of advanced real time systems and more conventional processing.

Among the real time applications are, for instance, the wanted persons system and the wanted vehicles system. There are approximately 350 telex units, and some 20 visual display units are linked to these countrywide systems. The systems are available 24 hours a day and at present deal with a query and updating frequency of around 7,000 calls per 24 hours.

Processing among more conventional lines includes, for example, systems for parking fines, breach of regulations fines, reports of crime, and passport matters.

In the field of criminal investigation certain records selector systems have been developed. Particularly worthy of mention is the trace finder system for fingerprints, where matters concerning identification of persons are on line and trace findings (from the scene of the crime) are carried out in batch processing. At present forty-nine people are employed in the computer unit. In addition the unit utilized the services of about ten consultants mainly for developmental work within the Judicial Information System (JIS) and the Criminal Records File (CRF), and for facilitating the flow of data to and from the CRF.

Equipment consists of two third-generation computers from the Honeywell Bull® 400 series and two communications computers. In addition to the normal equipment (punch card readers, high-speed printers, magnetic tape units, etc.), the computers are linked to mass storage. This is of the magnetic sheet type with a storage capacity of about 1.4 billion signs.

In June 1972 a contract was signed with Univac® concerning delivery of a very large and advanced computer system. Installation took place during the autumn of 1973.

The new system comprises a double computer system Univac 1110 with two communications computers. The disc storage capacity was increased to include 5 billion signs. About 300 visual display terminals will be connected in a countrywide network via five concentrators of the PDP-11 type. The computer system is dimensioned to handle thirteen queries per second in addition to considerable batch processing both centrally and via terminals. With the installation of the new computer system, the computer processing within the police department will be strongly directed toward on-line application, to a great extent a prerequisite for the replacement of certain local records requiring a large staff.

ADMINISTRATIVE DIVISION: This division handles the economic administration of the police. The division is divided into five sections:

1. FINANCE: This section is responsible for allocations and budgets, financial long-term planning, program budgets, and routines for central payments for the whole police system. Bookkeeping entries of some 40,000 items per month are effected by means of ADP.

2. PURCHASING involves the acquisition of material for the police and the National Forensic Science Laboratory. It is also responsible for selling discarded or rejected items.

3. *The Legal Section* handles contract, insurance, and compensation matters (although not salaries); and settlements of claims for damages and other matters where the board represents the Crown. This section also issues *Föreskrifter och Anvisningar för polisväsendet* (regulations and instruction for the police force).

4. *The Organization Section* deals with matters of local police organization, i.e. separation into police districts, subdistricts, etc., and matters concerning office equipment, as well as design and acquisition of forms. The annual police report is also compiled by this section.

5. *Office Service* supervises the board's premises and maintenance of its office equipment and furniture. It is also responsible for the reception and telephone exchange service within the National Swedish Police Board.

PERSONNEL DIVISION: The personnel division is divided into the following three sections. First, a general section deals with negotiations and interpretations of collective agreements and administrative statutes, and implementation of regulations. The second unit is responsible for the processing of appointments, dismissals, old age pensions, vacations, salary classification, etc.; and rules concerning personnel and vacation periods. Third, staff welfare deals with labor protection; occupational injuries; early retirement and disablement pensions; and all central activity concerning joint consultative committees, management, and staff welfare.

Under the supervision of the National Office for Administration Rationalization and Economy, the National Swedish Police Board and a number of police districts are trying a personnel administrative information system (PAI) for improved government personnel administration. A special work group within the staff section has the responsibility for this trial activity within the police system.

RECORDS DIVISION: This division is the latest addition within the National Swedish Police Board. It became operational on July 1, 1970.

The division is responsible for the various kinds of central crime records at the National Swedish Police Board. It is also responsible for large parts of an information system common to the whole judiciary information system. The records division is divided into the following areas:

1. *Control* deals with sentences, court orders, and fines from the entire country. It carries out the manual processing which pertains to ADP processing of these documents. This includes follow-up and ensures that summonses are approved and fines are paid. Information to various authorities regarding crimes and offences committed is distributed by this section. A new criminal records file constituting a technical coordination of the general criminal records and the National Swedish Police Board's criminal records came into use during 1973. The control section is now responsible for the input of information on crimes and criminals into this file.

2. *Data Processing* transfers information to be used in the various ADP systems to a computer input medium. This means that information is either punched on card or tape or transferred to magnetic tape.

3. *Central Police Records* keeps the National Swedish Police Board's police records, consisting of various subrecords

based on ADP techniques.

Criminal records contain information on persons sentenced for or suspected of crime and are based on the criminal files opened in the police districts. The criminal records section receives crime reports from the police districts and processes them to uncover a crime series, to chart the *modus operandi* of various criminals, and also to estimate official crime statistics. With the aid of the fingerprint center's records, tracing and identification can take place on a national basis. The publishing center issues from its own press *Polisunderrättelser* (police information) and a number of other publications for crime investigation. Moreover, there is a wanted persons system that makes it possible for inquires to be put through all police telex units and answers to be given directly to these units (on-line operation). The records center deals with extracts from the central police records. This section also operates a central passport records file, including all the country's 2.8 million passports. Personnel are on duty twenty-four hours a day at a coordination center which is in constant touch by telex with all police districts and is responsible for national and zone alerts and for operating an on-line system for searching for stolen vehicles.

The expansion of the National Swedish Police Board's records division makes it possible to use information stored in ADP systems for detection and investigative purposes to an ever increasing extent. There are already completed on-line systems for wanted persons and for searches for stolen motor vehicles. Thus, the police districts can get immediate information by telex about persons and vehicles of current interest, and at the same time the districts themselves can quickly alert the whole country or certain zones.

Security Department

The Security Department is immediately subordinate to the National Police Commissioner. The department exercises special police authority for the prevention and uncovering of crimes against national security. Activity is supervised by a head of department who takes the Deputy National Police Commissioner's place on the board when matters of security are under discussion. The security responsibility is divided as follows:

1. *Division A:* This unit is primarily concerned with prevention such as security and industrial protection, as well as control of personnel and special aliens. Security duties during state visits are also carried out by personnel from this preventive unit.
2. *Division B* carries out detection and investigative duties which include processing of security information.

The Security Department also includes regional security sections, in general linked to the counties. These sections are responsible directly to the department, but in certain cases personnel can be placed at the disposal of the county police commissioners.

SOCIAL COMMENTS

It would appear that the various components of the national police structure have been carefully streamlined to accomplish the functional objective of reform. Nevertheless, it is the personnel who animate the organization. The reputation and the status that the police enjoy in Swedish society not only reflect the educational level of the personnel but also their motivation. A political scientist examining another police system once stated that "it is generally accepted that the nature of police activities provides an important clue to the character of a political regime."[2] For this purpose the expression of public opinion by means of a representative sample has been the subject of a continuing exploration. At the base is a problem of values. Opinions can be shaped and manipulated. The majority can even be wrong if one prefers to believe author Henrik Ibsen in his play, *An Enemy of the People.*

A research survey initiated in 1974 by the Institute for Market Research (IMU), an independent Swedish counterpart of the Gallup Institute, raised the question of public perception of the trustworthiness of selected professional groups. At the same time the degree of influence of the various groups also was polled. A scale limit 1 to 7 was constructed, 1.0 indicating not trustworthy or having little influence and 7.0 equivalent to very trustworthy or having major influence.

Trustworthiness	*Mean*	*Influence*	*Mean*
Judges	5.9	The cabinet	6.0
Physicians	5.8	The legislature	6.0
Police officers	5.6	TV/Radio	5.4
Teachers	5.4	Business/Industry	5.3
Attorneys	5.1	Trade unions	5.3
Cabinet members	4.5	Courts of law	5.2
Civil servants	4.5	Banks	5.1
Trade union leaders	4.5	Newspapers	5.1
TV/Radio reporters	4.4	Police	4.9
Legislators	4.0	Teachers	4.3
Newspaper Journalists	3.2		

Note: N = 750.

An examination of the sample showed that women trusted the police more than men. Elderly persons and those with lower education placed more trust in the police than younger citizens and those with higher education. Different income levels appeared to have no significant impact. Women, elderly, and the lower educated assigned more influence to the police than men, youth, and those with a higher education.[3] In the light of this result it is imperative to examine the quality and the quantity of personnel who wish to embark on a police career. To the extent that occupational prestige is important, a Swedish random sample in 1958, prior to the police reform, listed twenty-five occupations with a police officer ranked as number sixteen:

Prestige Ratings of Twenty-five Occupations

Professor	1.5
Company director	1.6
Teacher, elementary, secondary*	1.9
Ship owner	1.9

Pharmacist	1.9
Head cashier	1.9
Colonel in the Armed Forces	2.0
Grocer, shop owner	2.1
Captain in merchant marine	2.2
Barber, independent or employer	2.3
Goldsmith, employee	2.3
Carpenter, independent or employer	2.3
Accountant	2.4
Typographer	2.8
Taxicab owner	2.8
Policeman	2.8
Shop salesman	2.9
Noncommissioned officers in Armed Forces	2.9
Building laborer	2.9
Traveling salesman	3.0
Actor	3.0
Waiter	3.1
Postman	3.2
Tailor, employee	3.2
Shoe-shiner	4.2

*Primary and secondary school teachers were given the same rating.
NOTE: N = 1700.

SOURCE: Gösta Carlsson, *Social Mobility and Class Structure* (Lund: CWK Gleerup, (1958)), p. 148. Study originally done by SIFO.

What we see in Sweden is a great emphasis on occupation and specialized education as conveyors of prestige rather than wealth. It is clear that occupations in the civil service, particularly those requiring a university education, bestow greater prestige in Swedish as compared with American society.

Those in the military, both officers and enlisted men, probably have more prestige than they do in the United States in spite of the fact that Sweden has not been involved in a war for nearly 160 years. They, too, are employed by the government. This is probably true also of policemen, even though they are employed by lower levels of government.

In Sweden, there is not the prestige differential between theoretical and generalist work as compared with technical and applied work that one finds in England and to a lesser degree in the United States. Highly skilled technical workers have more prestige than in the United States.[4]

A random population sample of 1,000 by IMU in February 1973 asked the question "How much education do you believe is required to become a police officer?" Nearly 40 percent thought that police officers should possess a secondary school education or above (which is roughly equivalent to two years of American college—associate of arts or science degree). Responding to another question in the same poll 80 percent believed that the police conduct themselves correctly in their interaction with members of the public. It would be unusual for the police to use unnecessary coercion. It should be noted that the youths in the larger cities were inclined to view police behavior as somewhat more coercive.

In response to an official inquiry about police education in Stockholm in 1972, several authorities who were consulted considered that completed secondary school education ought to be the general minimum requirement for recruitment of the police.[5] The National Police Board concurred and held that the time has come to increase the educational entrance requirement. About the same time the Chief of the Training Division stated that the recruiting base had improved to the extent that a police recruit today had a better education than the average Swede.[6]

As to the personal qualities that were most desirable for a police officer, the random sample referred to above listed the following priorities: 80 to 85 percent of the respondents stated calmness, judgment, understanding, humaneness, and self-discipline; 70 to 75 percent stated effectiveness, decisiveness, firmness, cooperation, empathy, and initiative; and 45 percent indicated authority and intelligence.

When separating people in rural and urban areas, the inhabitants in the large cities were somewhat less positive, nearly 5 to 10 percent lower. The distinction between rural and urban opinion is notable in another poll conducted in 1968 in which only 62 percent of rural dwellers but 73 percent of urban dwellers wanted more police. Forty-nine percent would like increased authority for the police while 44 percent thought that the police had sufficient authority and power.[7]

A brief glance at the statistics shows that 653,984 offenses were reported to the police in 1972. The city of Malmö, population 315,118, accounted for 46,064 complaints or 146 per 1,000 inhabitants. Stockholm, population 723,688, showed 104,993 complaints or 145 per 1,000 population; and Gothenburg, population 499,723, had 51,003 complaints or 102 per 1,000 population.[8]

RECRUITMENT AND TRAINING

In Sweden there is a distinction between the police officer's career and the police chief's career. While courses at the central police school and the national academy normally qualify one for promotion, a university degree in law is required for appointments of the police chief and to higher positions with the National Police Board. Dispensation has been granted to a small number of senior officers for duty in some minor police districts. In these cases a university course in criminal law and procedure has been deemed sufficient. Some police officers are part-time students of law.

At the police chief's course starting in January of 1974, ten were police officers having a law degree; ten others, three of whom were women, were civilians with law degrees. The course lasts for six months and comprises police organization and administration, leadership functions, planning and control, personnel management, and general police duties. The graduates thereafter perform as practitioners for two years, normally in middle management with six months at a local police district, three months with the county administration, three months with the prosecutor, and twelve months with a law court. The candidates are then called back to the police academy for a two-month theoretical course followed by four months of practice at the National Police Board. While awaiting vacancies the candidates frequently are employed as assistants to police chiefs.

A young man or woman who sets out to become a police officer must be a Swedish citizen, have an aptitude for police work, be of good character, be at least nineteen, and possess an automobile driving license. A complete medical examination must satisfy requirements according to a set form. The wearing of glasses or contact lenses will disqualify. Applicants above the age of thirty are not accepted.

Because of the relatively small number of applicants during 1972 and 1973 (only 634 or 35 percent of 1,801 applicants were accepted), it has not been feasible to require graduation from secondary school. Both the local and regional police authorities are engaged in recruiting, interviewing, and processing suitable candidates to the recruiting section of the National Police Board. The educational background of the 634 recruits showed the following data:[9]

Secondary school examination (or university entrance exam)	38.9	percent
Vocational school examination	16.6	”
High school examination	8.2	”
Two-year folk high school (community college)	12.3	”
Police cadet training school	12.2	”
Military reserve officers' school	0.5	”
Primary or basic school (9 years)	10.7	”
Other	0.6	”
	100.0	percent

Inquiries and preliminary applications are screened by the recruitment section. A standard application form subsequently is mailed to the police chief in the district of the applicant. The local police collect background information from a variety of sources. If the outcome is promising the applicant is invited to an interview by the local police. The complete file is forwarded to the National Police Board with the police chief's suggestions for acceptance or rejection. Those accepted are employed as extra or probationary police officers. They will attend the basic police course of forty weeks, forty hours per week, in Ulriksdal near Stockholm (See Table IV). Recruits are accepted three times a year. The spacious training grounds contains a cafeteria, lecture halls, recreational facilities for sport and play, and various technical installations in order that theoretical and practical instruc-

TABLE IV
POLICE ACADEMY CURRICULA (1973)

TOPIC/SUBJECT	Number of hours in courses:				
	1	2	3	4	5
General police knowledge	608	131	188	217	379
Uniform police:					
General surveillance	142	28	44	69	82
Special surveillance	40	22	3	39	69
Traffic law and enforcement:					
General	134				26
Special			3	9	18
Criminal investigation and detective duties:					
General investigation	114	51	64	42	56
Special investigation			2	4	28
Criminal intelligence:					
General	9		8	18	
Special	16		10	22	
Criminalistics:					
General	52	21	48		34
Special		3	6	4	20
Communications	37				
Firearms training and policy	34				22
Penal law	71	32	68	40	
Special penal law	27	66	32	16	57
Road traffic legislation	*	36	20	16	28
Public order legislation	14	14	9	16	14
Food legislation	2				7
Alcoholic beverage legislation	6	10	3		8
Aliens legislation	2				
Narcotic legislation		2			
The firearms ordinance	2	2			
Civil law	35	26	40		
Judicial procedure	19				
Administration and management			3	61	84
Police legislation				4	
Prosecution and execution of sentences					4
Police authority actions				31	38
Working conditions				10	
Personnel management				5	23
Finance administration				4	15
Personnel welfare activities				5	
Information and public relations				3	
Municipal law and administrative law					
Electronic data knowledge			3		
Premises and equipment					

TABLE IV—(Cont'd.)

TOPIC/SUBJECT	Number of hours in courses:				
	1	2	3	4	5
Bookkeeping and accounting			32		
Swedish language	62				
English language	40				
Social science	54	14		10	40
Sociology					22
Psychology & psychiatry	46	36		57	44
Psychology	34	24		42	22
Psychiatry	12	12		15	22
Medicine	32		18	28	42
First aid	26				
Social medicine					10
Forensic medicine	6		18	28	32
Motor vehicle proficiency	83				
Office and technical equipment	40				
Physical training	144	18	16	28	45
Baton techniques	50	6	3	6	12
Swimming and rescue	16	2	2	4	4
Leadership			14	**	**

*Subject is dealt with under general police knowledge.
**Work supervision for commanders and chiefs is included in psychology.

1 = Basic Course
2 = Advanced Course
3 = Captain's Course
4 = Commander's Course
5 = Police Chief's Course

tion can flow uninterrupted. Upon completion of the course the recruits serve approximately two years in the various divisions of a police department under the guidance of an experienced police officer before they are eligible for regular appointment. Placement depends on vacancies in the local police districts. After having served about five years a police officer is summoned to a ten-weeks general course at the police academy in Solna north of Stockholm. At the academy the participants must provide for his own accommodations. Both the instructors and the students wear civilian clothes. Normal instruction lasts from 8 A.M. to 4 P.M.

The ranks of the Swedish police are as follows:

Poliskonstapel	patrol officer
Första poliskonstapel	police sergeant
Polis/Kriminal-assistent	police lieutenant
Första polis/kriminal-assistent	senior lieutenant
Polis/kriminal-inspektör	police captain
Polis kommissarie	precinct commander
Polis intendent	assistant police chief
Polis överintendent	deputy police chief
Polismästare	police chief

At the National Police Board there are, in addition, functional titles such as bureau director, bureau chief, branch chief, and other indicating responsibilities. Women police officers complete the same training as their male colleagues. They also perform the initial duties in uniform. Eventually nearly all of them end up in plain clothes as detectives and social and juvenile officers. Both training centers have a faculty of full-time instructors; police officers; and professionals from other disciplines, i.e. forensic scientists, attorneys, pathologists, psychiatrists, and psychologists.

The system of advancement in rank differs considerably from the situation in England and the United States. In practice promotion below *Polis/kriminal-inspektör* (captain) is broadly based on seniority if the course work has been completed. A potential captain must attend a course focusing on middle management, leadership, tactical problem-solving, and various planning and administrative tasks. For those whose education and performance make them competitive for the position of *Kommissarie* (commander) or for a higher one, a special course is required. In addition to police theory, advanced administration, and personnel management, there are lectures in fiscal and legal problems. There are about 140 specialized courses held every year at the two learning centers, i.e. crime and criminal investigation, traffic and vehicle control, automotive driving, physical training, self-defense, firearms proficiency, and rescue operations for accidents and disasters. Dogs are extensively used for police purposes, and canine police courses are conducted jointly with the military in an army compound.

What is the social strata from which the police draw their manpower? A study of recruitment to Stockholm's police district beginning in 1967 and continuing through 1972 revealed the following:[10]

Occupation of father:

Academician and high-ranking civil servant	4.5 percent
Peasant, farmer	25.9 percent
Craftsman, civil servant, businessman	39.4 percent
Laborer	25.5 percent
Police officer	4.7 percent
	100 percent

The current strength of the police is above 14,000 with a ratio of approximately 1.7 per 1,000 population. In Stockholm the ratio is 2.6 police per 1,000 population. In addition, there are 3,000 clerical, technical, and administrative employees. For emergency and war situations there exists a reserve police. To relieve police from routine guard duties, a semiofficial organization called ABAB provides uniformed security men to watch embassies and foreign missions in major cities. To encourage the interest of youth in the police, the vocational schools in Lund and Stockholm have included a two-year police option in their curricula. However, they do not contribute significantly to police recruitment.

The technological level of the Swedish police is superb, as can be seen in computer techniques and air and sea policing. Six of the seven helicopters of the National Police Board also cover ambulance service inside land and territorial waters. Mobile police stations have been tested in various regions.

As to the cost factors it is difficult to make international comparisons because of the social and fiscal allocation of currency. However, compared to the cost per taxpayer the expenditures are nearly double what they are in the neighboring country of Norway in 1972: Forty dollars per Swedish taxpayer go to the police, compared to twenty dollars in Norway.

A police officer in Sweden carries an automatic pistol as part of his personal police equipment. His colleagues in Norway and England are not equipped with firearms during the routine performance of their duties.

Possibly the need of the police in Sweden to carry a weapon is related to the increase in reported crimes from 300,000 in 1963 to about 530,000 in 1970. Criminal patterns have become both more violent and more complex. With the number of motor vehicles doubling since 1960, complicated traffic problems have resulted. The overall percentage of offenses solved by the police average forty-five, while crimes listed in the Penal Code show a clearance rate of 34 percent.[11]

The deployment of personnel can be distinguished from the approach taken in a well-known American text on police administration.[12] This is illustrated by a Swedish chart of July 1, 1972 as follows:

Uniformed branches:		*Investigative branches:*	
Secretarial & clerical	375	Crime intelligence section	897
Patrol services	6,341	General investigation	805
Traffic services	1,358	Criminal investigation	2,018
Temporary employees	1,768	Scene of crime (evidence) technicians	263

With the prevailing philosophy of personnel management in the public services, the base pay as well as the prospects of increased earnings come with seniority and qualifications. In middle management and below there is less emphasis on competitive endeavor than in England and the United States. Monetary incentives, as well as favorable working conditions, are important factors in the motivation of personnel and have reduced the turnover of manpower. Credit for the improved work climate should go to the Swedish Police Association that organizes over 90 percent of the police officers. The association has bargaining powers, and its board members participate in all important inquiries pertaining to the police. Since the pay and working conditions of public servants are the outcome of periodical collective bargaining, four major associations have been recognized by the government as legitimate agents. There has been occasional critical disagreement between the government and the police which resulted in so-called "blue flu" in Stockholm in the 1950's. Collective bargaining has been more conciliatory in recent years, and fact-finding committees and mediation are standard procedure. Special provisions have been made in collective contracts to prevent strikes in essential sectors such as defense, public safety, and health. The settlement of wages for public servants in principle is governed by the same procedure that applies to the private production sector. The bargaining power has been delegated to the Governmental Negotiation Authority *(Statens Avtalsverk)*.

The impact of laymen and politicians on policing through representation on central and local boards has been mentioned previously. Pursuant to the recommendation by the Swedish Crime Commission Report of 1973,[13] a greater emphasis should be placed on the reduction of disturbances of the peace and crime through a vigorous community relations effort by the police. Without becoming bogged down in such an ambiguous concept as crime causation, there are many ways to discover and contain potential crimes. The saying that each society has the police it deserves should not be an argument for the police to ignore their obligation to initiate and improve police-public interaction. It is an acknowledged fact that the mechanization of police operations has increased the distance between police and the public. The claim has been made that routine cruising of patrol cars has no effect on crime.[14] Team, unit beat, and neighborhood policing have been responses to this phenomenon in British and American cities. The Swedish response has been area or neighborhood police and community liaison officers working in uniform or plain clothes as necessary from the precinct stations. Their ability to establish friendly contacts with the youth has been a crucial factor. In order to reach out for those age groups who are most susceptible, the police cooperate with community schools and actively participate in the instruction of pupils on such subjects as traffic safety, criminal law, and justice, which have become required topics in Swedish schools. The concern for the young is logical as long as a disproportionate share, around 70 percent, of the crimes are committed by youths between the ages of fifteen and twenty-four. In Sweden no one may be sentenced to a sanction for a crime he committed before he reached fifteen years of age, according to the Penal Code, Chapter 33, Section 1.

Community sport clubs, scout and church movements, other voluntary associations, and parent meetings are important targets for police interaction. Relevant information to the public is another matter where the National Police Board has attempted to mobilize the interest of the mass media, television, radio, and the press. Television and radio are state-controlled corporations ruled by independent boards. The police efforts here, however, have been a mixed blessing, mainly due to the caustic attitude of the television leadership. Mobile police exhibitions have been shown to attract interest. Since the population is largely homogeneous the police have not been particularly concerned with minority groups. In recent years, however, tens of thousands of laborers from countries with cultures very different from Sweden's have been admitted. This fact also has had an impact on crime patterns, narcotic traffic, and violent crime in particular.

Police distribution of crime protection pamphlets and close cooperation with the insurance companies have made the public aware of means other than firearms to protect their families and property. Reduced insurance rates benefited people who took care to install the safety devices in their homes and cars which were prescribed by the insurance firms. Reinforced police surveillance of subway, bus, and railroad stations, frequently through the use of television cameras, has been initiated.

Banks, post offices, and firms dealing in valuables have been advised about appropriate safeguards. In big cities hardware crime prevention is essential, and individuals as well as industry and business, are rendered gratis assistance by police advisory units. In spite of all the emphasis on preventive measures, it cannot be denied that the crime rate during the last few decades has risen more than the population has increased, a phenomenon consistent with the trend in other western societies.

The effectiveness of the detective component subsequently is called into question. As in other democratic countries the capacity of the police to solve crimes and have the defendants convicted must be considered in the context of the criminal procedure. The trend has been to place great emphasis on individual rights and privacy which virtually means that the discretionary powers of police in the areas of arrest, search, and seizure have been carefully circumscribed. Police questioning with a view of obtaining confessions has become controversial. Subsequently, greater emphasis than ever before is being placed upon physical evidence. This has stimulated the interest in criminalistics. Even with the greatly expanded formal police training in Sweden, it is unrealistic to expect all police officers to locate and collect evidence according to approved methods. Thus, crime scene investigators or evidence technicians and forensic science laboratories are playing increasingly important roles in modern detective work. Evidence of crime, which in the past has passed unchallenged, today is likely to be carefully scrutinized both in form and substance. As previously mentioned the examination and presentation of many types of evidence are now independent of the Swedish police.

THE SWEDISH NATIONAL LABORATORY OF FORENSIC SCIENCE[15]

In 1964 the laboratory division of the former National Institute for Criminalistics was reorganized (see Figure 3) and named the National Laboratory of Forensic Science. The laboratory has the following tasks:

1. Forensic laboratory investigations are conducted on behalf of criminal courts, prosecutors, and police authorities. The laboratory also accepts requests from defense attorneys, private individuals, and other government branches on a fee basis.

2. A study of the literature and the development of new methods within the various disciplines of forensic science and technology is carried out.

3. Law and science are taught at the University of Stockholm. Teaching assignments at police training centers are also accepted.

It is further planned to carry out applied research in forensic science. Currently the staff numbers seventy-five, six of whom have Ph.D.s and twenty, masters and bachelors of science. The location, collection, and forwarding of criminal evidence in the field are routinely handled by the local police authorities. In some cases such as fires, the examination of vegetation and soil conditions, and certain violent crimes, the laboratory has dispatched experts. About thirty of the larger police districts have technical

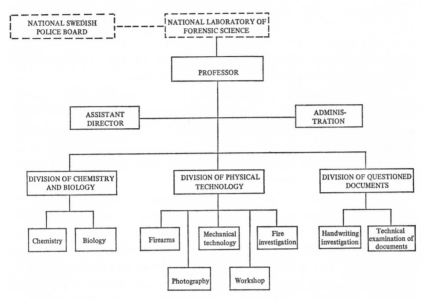

Figure 3. The National Swedish Laboratory of Forensic Science, 1972.

squads. Three of the major cities, i.e. Stockholm, Gothenburg, and Malmö have police laboratories for the analyses of less complicated matters. The homicide squad of the National Criminal Investigation Department relies heavily upon the police laboratory of Stockholm. It may expedite scientific examination by securing and classifying fingerprints at the same location. The police laboratory also examines toolmarks and firearms.

The increasing weight placed on time in modern detective work has caused all modern police forces to utilize electronic computers for the transmission of messages. Legal requirements often necessitate fast verification of identity. The criminal justice system, therefore, enlists the expertise of forensic pathology and odontology. Sweden has a medical examiner system comprising six regional governmental institutes for this purpose. About 9,000 autopsies are performed each year. Toxicological analyses are performed by the Government Laboratory for Forensic Chemistry. The workload is some 4,000 analyses per year. This institute also analyzes some 20,000 yearly cases of suspected driving under the influence of liquor and performs blood and urine tests. Another activity is serological tests in all cases of questioned paternity. The National Laboratory of Forensic Science takes charge of all other matters, sometimes assisted by specialists from other institutes and universities. Some typical tasks are the following:

The examination of handwriting on checks, last wills, anonymous letters, contracts, and forms is performed by six officials. Two others carry out technical investigation of typed and printed texts of bank notes, checks, driver licenses, passports, stamps, and paintings. Other examinations pertain to ball-point, paste, paper, printing inks, and the reconstruction of erased texts.

Three officials are busy with systems analysis and individualization of bullets, cartridges, and firearms; calculation of ballistics; and the determination of shooting distance. They participate in the reconstruction of accidents and crimes involving firearms and furthermore, in the identification of explosives and their impacts.

Mechanical technology is handled by four officials. This broad field includes *inter alia* comparative analysis of toolmarks, shoe imprints, gloves, locks, motor vehicle parts, and coins (counterfeits). Officials participate in the reconstruction of industrial and marine accidents.

The cost of fires in terms of life and money is critical in complex society. Arson is a crime that has been on the increase, and six officials investigate a variety of chemical, mechanical, and electrical causes of fires; describe fire damages; and reconstruct the initial phases of fires in fire test rooms.

In the field of chemistry the analyses of drugs (including narcotics) have increased much. The section has fifteen officials and deals with a wide range of materials, the most common of which may be glass, paint flakes, clothes (for locating suspicious microsubstances from crime scenes), metal beads from welding operations (safecracking), and oil spill in the sea.

The biology section of ten officials currently has most work with the analysis of cannabis and opium (in conjunction with the chemistry section). Other typical examinations pertain to blood, blood spots, blood grouping, the analysis of sperm and saliva (including bloodgrouping), as well as urine. Again biological analyses cover a very wide field of expertise.

The photography section of four members performs documentation work for the other sections.

The laboratory maintains a representative reference collection of items ranging from counterfeit bills and drugs to firearms and munition. The library comprises 5,000 volumes and more than 90 periodicals. The location is the city of Linköping, some 130 miles south of Stockholm.

The international reputation of Swedish police and forensic science is well established, partly due to the influence of Doctor Harry Söderman, Arne Svensson, and Otto Wendel, whose books have been translated into many languages. The reform of the criminal justice system with particular reference to the police has been a realistic approach to the problem of maintaining a high level of public satisfaction combined with social order. This removes the sense of tension and urgency which too often characterizes some aspects of police operations in other countries.

Compared to the annual expenditures on police in earlier years, the new organization is costly. The investment in new buildings, motor vehicles, and equipment has been heavy, considering the rather expensive up-to-date apparatus required by modern forensic science. After assessing organizational development police leadership tends to stress the advantages of forming larger units by the amalgamation of police districts. It is proposed to initiate a further reduction in the number of police districts from 119 to 90. The structure and the impact of police reform have aroused much curiosity. Every year the National Police Board has visitors from all over the world. This is also reflected in articles in foreign police journals.

FOOTNOTES

[1]Brian Chapman, *Profession of Government: The Public Service in Europe* (London: Allen and Unwin, 1959) , p. 50.

[2]David H. Bayley, *The Police and Political Development in India* (Princeton: Princeton University Press, 1969) , p. 52.

[3]*Svensk Polis*, No. 3, 1974; official monthly magazine of the National Police Board.

[4]Richard F. Tomasson, *Sweden: Prototype of Modern Society* (New York: Random House, 1970) , pp. 226-227.

[5]*Polisen i Stockholm*, October 1972. A report by the Ministry of Justice.

[6]*Svensk Polis*, No. 10, 1972.

[7]*Svensk Polis,* No. 8, 1968.

[8]*Svensk Polis,* No. 3, 1973.

[9]Gunilla Cedermark, *Selection and Training of Police Personnel in England, France, and Sweden.* A 1970 Criminology Research Study. Strasbourg: Council of Europe, mimeographed.

[10]Gunilla Cedermark and Hans Klette, *Polis; Myndighet—Manniska* (Lund: Studentlitteratur, 1973), p. 115.

[11]Nelson, p. 69.

[12]O. W. Wilson, *Police Administration* (New York: McGraw-Hill Book Co., 1963).

[13]*Betankande avgivet av brottskommissionen, Justitiedepartemantet,* Stockholm, 1973.

[14]G. L. Kelling et al.: *The Kansas City Preventive Patrol Experiment* (Washington, D.C.: Police Foundation, 1974).

[15]Andreas Maehly, The Swedish National Laboratory of Forensic Science, Solna 1974, unpublished paper.

CHAPTER 5

THE JUDICIARY—PROSECUTION, DEFENSE, AND THE COURTS

HISTORY OF THE JUDICIARY

IN MODERN CRIMINAL JUSTICE a distinction is made between the function of examination and that of prosecution. The character and place of criminal investigation and prosecution in the institutional framework display considerable variations among nations. Historically, the prosecution of offenders has evolved from private to public action. Since the time of Montesquieu (1689-1755) western democratic society is usually thought to be composed of three principal elements: the executive, the legislative, and the judiciary. The police department is an executive organization. Prosecutors and defense attorneys today are more often considered servants of the courts of justice. The establishment of a separate prosecutorial authority is a combination of evolution and adoption in legal tradition.

In republican Rome public prosecution allegedly was instituted by Calpurnius Piso, praetor in 211 B.C. Murder was one of the first crimes where the state assumed the responsibility for apprehension, examination, prosecution, adjudication, and compensation. These were the responsibilities of officials of the criminal court. Gradually, the urban prefect assumed responsibility for processing several types of criminals. During the Feudal Era, through Enlightenment, and beyond, the combination of functions in the office equivalent to a police chief today was common in Europe. The official supervised the investigation, acted as prosecutor, participated in the pronunciation of the sentence, and executed it. France, being a pertinent illustration of the gradual emergence of a unitary political system, witnessed the conscious efforts of the monarchs to control the machinery of justice. In the early thirteenth century the king deemed it necessary to protect his financial interests through a representative in the feudal courts. An ordinance of 1539 makes reference to the *procureur du roi* who appeared as an official charged with the preservation of public order and the repression of crime.

The police reform in France in 1667—a result of law revisions—effected some separation between police and judicial functions. Since the Revolution of 1789 most European countries imitated French public administration blended with Prussian elements. Code Napoleon (the criminal procedure of 1808) contained a mixture of accusatory and inquisitorial principles. The reintroduction of the accusatory procedure stimulated adversary proceedings and the rise of the modern prosecutors and defenders:

> The criminal law of almost every nation has begun with the accusatory procedure, and has changed to the inquisitorial procedure. As evolution in an opposite direction, however, is now apparent; everywhere there is a tendency to restore the essential safeguards of the accusatory system, publicity and confrontation. The only institution of the inquisitorial system which has defied criticism, and which is probably more powerful and general than ever, is that of the public prosecutor.[1]

PROSECUTION

In the Nordic countries written provincial laws were compiled in the Middle Ages. Probably the first written Swedish law was the Code of Uppland enacted in 1296. Based on customary law it was drafted by a group of lawmen who had contact with Swedish scholars of Roman law from the University of Bologna; comparative research has a long tradition in Sweden. Little is known about the prosecutor in the pre-modern period though comprehensive codes were compiled in the fourteenth, fifteenth, and eighteenth centuries. Procedural parts were embodied in the Code of 1734: "From time to time parliament approved a number of piecemeal revisions of procedural rules, but plans for overall reform failed to win legislative acceptance until the 20th century."[2]

↓ The formal authority governing the functions of the prosecutor is found in the Code of Judicial Procedure of 1942 and the Instruction for Public Prosecution Authorities Act of 1964. Criminal cases can be prosecuted by the state as well as by private individuals. In the latter case Chapter 47, Section 1 of the code states that an injured person who desires to institute a prosecution shall file with the court a written application for a summons against the person to be charged. It must contain the identity of the defendant, the criminal act, the plaintiff's claim, and the evidence offered.

The following excerpts of the code will highlight the contemporary scene:

> Chapter 20, Section 1: No issue of criminal liability may be entertained by the court unless a prosecution for the offense has been instituted. . . .
>
> Section 2: Unless otherwise prescribed, public prosecutors have standing to prosecute for offenses falling within the domain of public prosecution. As to the standing of exceptional prosecutors to prosecute for offenses falling within the domain of public prosecution, especially enacted provisions shall apply. Prosecutors may appeal to a higher court even for the benefit of the suspect.[3]

The prosecutorial authority is organized under the Ministry of Justice with a Chief State Prosecutor *(Riksåklagare)* and his secretariat. The territorial structure comprises county prosecutors for exceptional cases, three principal prosecutors in the major cities (Stockholm, Gothenburg and Malmö), twenty-one county prosecutors, and eighty-seven district prosecutors. Depending on the work load a number of assistant prosecutors may be found at the various levels in the hierarchy. Each prosecuting district should support at least three prosecutors. A government committee report of 1970 proposed a consolidation which would reduce the number of prosecutor districts to eighty-one. Compared to the situation in other countries, several characteristics are apparent: Prosecutions are organized as a hierarchy at three levels; the personnel has civil service status and holds tenure. A university law degree is mandatory. The degree probably compares to an American J.D. rather than to an LL.B., and more than two years of practical training as the assistant of a district judge is required. There is a formal distinction between the district prosecutors and their superiors, referred to as state prosecutors. The latter are appointed by the king, which in practice means the cabinet. No consent or confirmation by the Parliament is required. In the performance of their duties the prosecutors are accountable to the Parliamentary ombudsman. The Chief State Prosecutor submits annual reports to the ombudsman, known as commissioner of justice (JO). The latter also supervises the courts of law, the police, and the armed forces. The most recent annual report of the commissioner of justice showed that of 357 cases investigated by the ombudsman, twenty-nine pertained to public prosecutors. In addition, the commissioner personally undertakes random inspections of prosecutors' offices. Since the vast majority of prosecutions is initiated by the public prosecutors, the victims of criminal attacks often expect the prosecutor to look after their interests. The law allows private claims resulting from a crime to be pursued in conjunction with trial of the criminal. The claims may be based on property damage, monetary loss, or personal injuries—medical expenses and lost income because of inability to work. No statistics are available to clarify this issue; however, it is suspected that prosecutors may hesitate to include claims if they complicate the prosecuting task. In such cases the victim has recourse to civil action, which is not realistic, partly because of the financial state of the defendant and the elaborate and time-consuming procedure.

The chief state prosecutor is the general accuser in the Supreme Court. State and district prosecutors appear in the lower courts and the courts of appeal. Furthermore, the chief state prosecutor is obliged to initiate actions in lower and appeal courts when crimes in public office have been committed by top civil servants and judges or by military commanders, e.g. bribery, illicit rewards, and divulgence of secrets detrimental to national security. When an offense has been reported and there is sufficient cause to assume that it falls within the purview of public prosecution, a preliminary investigation is initiated by the police or the prosecutor. The National Police Board in consultation with the chief state prosecutor has drawn up the procedural details. Normally, the prosecutor directs the investigation of difficult or serious cases. In practice, however, specialization makes police more competent to cope with the great variety of criminal behavior patterns. The police officer in charge keeps the prosecutor continually informed. The aim of the preliminary investigation is to determine whom to charge with a crime. The law points out that the investigation should be conducted so that no person is unnecessarily exposed to suspicion, or put to unnecessary expense or inconvenience. Both damaging and favorable circumstances shall be considered. Any person who is thought to possess relevant information may be examined and can be subpoenaed for examination if the distance is no more than 30 kilometers (18.6 miles).

A police officer may invite anyone found at the scene of an offense to immediately accompany him to the nearest police station for questioning. The police may use coercion in case of recalcitrant behavior. This measure is not defined as arrest, but as detention, and is limited to six hours. For years this has been a convenient police practice which was finally legalized in the Code of Judicial Procedure of 1942. Similar provisions exist in the other Nordic countries.

Every suspect has a right to have a trusted person (defense counsel) present during a police interrogation. Without permission of the investigating authority, no person present at an examination may speak to the person being questioned during the interrogation. When the preliminary investigation indicates that a person might reasonably be suspected, that person must be informed of the suspicion. The defense counsel will be informed about the result of the investigation as soon as this can be done without detriment to the case. Following the completion of the preliminary investigation, the prosecutor must decide whether or not to process the case to trial. By comparison, in France the examining magistrate, not the prosecutor, decides whether the case should be tried or dismissed. In neither case is a grand jury summoned. In the United Kingdom this apparatus for indictment was abolished in 1933. The grand jury still survives as an important procedural tool in the United States. A Swedish prosecution, once instituted, may not be amended, and the prosecutor will apply to the court for a summons against the defendant. The principle of legality governing prosecutions precludes the practice of plea bargaining, though the charge shall be consolidated if it involves several defendants or offenses. Practically all information from the police investigation is revealed and documented during the court preliminary examination. Any additional informaton also is released to the defense attorney who has had access to the complete police file of his client. Subsequently, the element of surprise is conspicuously absent at the trial, a feature different from the trial scene in the United States. When a court hearing takes place the indigent offender will be assigned a lawyer, often a public defender. Offenses punishable by fines only do not require preliminary court hearings. In this case arrest may not occur. On the other hand, a felony punishable by imprisonment of a minimum of two years will result in the suspect being taken into custody unless it is evident that there is no cause for it.

The law differentiates between *arrest (anhållande)*, usually on warrant by the investigating authority or the prosecutor; *apprehension (gripande)*, where immediate action is taken by the police with or without a warrant; and *detention, (häkting)*, initiated by the prosecutor. The law imposes a 24-hour limit on police arrests before the suspect is brought before a magistrate. However, when an application for a detention order has been made, the prosecutor has four days to prepare for the initial court hearing. The magistrate, upon concluding the hearing, must pronounce his decision whether or not to keep the suspect in custody. If the suspect is taken into custody the reasons must be given, as well as a time limit set. Bail is rarely granted by Swedish courts since there is no constitutional right to be free on bail. Search and seizure warrants are issued by the police authority, the prosecutor, or the court. Frequently detectives search premises after they obtain the consent of the suspect or when a delay entails risks. The law has outlined the detailed conditions pertaining to search and seizure. Since the concept of exclusionary rule is notably absent in Sweden it serves little purpose to go into the procedural technicalities, which belong in a legal textbook. It should be mentioned that the frisking of a suspect is a routine matter even if the risk factor is of no major concern, such as in the United States. Also if the frisking leads to the discovery of anything that can be used to prove criminal activity, such things are seized as lawful evidence. If the police or the prosecution find it necessary to call upon professional experts, such as forensic scientists, pathologists, dentists, and psychiatrists, the court may act on its own. Before appointing experts, the judge invites the prosecutor and the defense attorney to state their views. Occasionally the defending counsel engages experts to back up his position.

At the trial or main hearing the prosecutor will state his charge upon which the defendant is asked to enter a plea of guilty or not guilty. Thereafter, the prosecution unfolds its case by giving the particulars upon which the case is based. The hearing is public and the proceedings oral. The prosecutor's role at the trial does not differ significantly from that of his counterparts in the United States, France, or Germany. In theory he plays a nonpolitical part. Cross-examinations, as they are known in British and American courts, are not practiced. In his presentation of evidence he does not have to weigh carefully procedural limitations known as exclusionary rules in American criminal justice. As previously mentioned, the imposition of fines is the common device of adjudicating criminals. While the authority of the police officer to fine a violator is carefully circumscribed, the public prosecutor has more leeway. Nevertheless, his authority is restricted to offenses for which only a fine can be imposed. A further limitation is given in the requirement that the defendant in writing enter a plea of guilt and accept the fine. The fining by the prosecutor is limited to forty day-fines. In Sweden the age of consent is fifteen. Delinquents below this age are referred directly to the child welfare board for action. Regarding juvenile delinquents between the ages of fifteen and twenty-one the prosecutor in certain cases at his discretion may waive preliminary court hearings and allow the local child welfare board the responsibility for the disposal of the young persons for the purpose of rehabilitation.

THE DEFENSE

There is no obligation to employ legal aid in Swedish court proceedings. In practice, however, lawyers represent clients in civil and criminal cases. An attorney appearing in court as defense counsel must be a Swedish citizen residing in the country. In exceptional cases the court may grant permission to individuals who do not meet these qualifications. If a criminal defendant has not hired his own attorney the court will appoint a defense counsel. The attorney must be a member of the Swedish Bar Association. This requirement is certified by the procedural law, Chapter 8, Section 1, which states: "There shall be a general association of advocates for the realm. The charter of the association shall be ratified by the King. An advocate is one who is a member of the association." If a criminal court has been unable to appoint a voluntary defense counsel, an attorney having his office in the district is obliged to accept the task of public defense. In order to understand the role of the defense in Sweden, it is worth observing that the court has supreme control over the evaluation of evidence as well as the way it was procured. Also, the court has the power to call on expert opinion. These important features may limit the opportunities of the defense attorney to challenge the evidence. The suspect must attend the preparatory court hearing and the main hearing in person. The defense attorney will be present to assist him. As to the assessment of the mental and emotional state of the defendant, the test of normality is not usually raised by the defense. Any doubt on the part of the police or the prosecution as to the capacity of the defendant will result in a request to the court to appoint psychiatric experts. Their medical diagnosis will determine whether or not the defendant is capable of standing trial. (The legal definition of insanity based on the M'Naghten "right and wrong" test is unknown in the Nordic countries.) The Penal Code of 1965 states that for a crime committed by a person with a mental disease, feeblemindedness, or other mental abnormality, no other sanction may be applied than surrender for special care in accord with the Mental Health Act. Self-induced intoxication is no defense. Since the defense attorney should be aware of all aspects of the case having a bearing on its outcome, he can challenge matters of fact and of law and question the victim, the defendant, and the witnesses, including expert witnesses. If his client is kept in custody the attorney can claim privileged communication. In Sweden as in some other countries, the defense tends to focus on circumstantial evidence. When the prosecutor and the defense counsel have stated their positions the court will withdraw in order to reach the verdict. In the absence of a jury the ability of the defense to plead by persuasion is probably limited in terms of impact, compared to the situation in countries having the traditional trial by jury system. Questions of fact and of law are answered by majority rule by the court composed of juridical experts and assessors. When the sentence has been pronounced by the judge the defense counsel, as well as the prosecutor, can file petitions for regular appeal within three weeks. The appeal petition must specify

1. the judgment being appealed;
2. the grounds for the appeal, stating why the appellant considers the fact-finding and legal conclusions of the lower court to be erroneous; and
3. the particular part of the judgment attacked and the change in the judgment demanded by the appellant.

Furthermore, the appellant must specify the evidence upon which he relies and indicate what he intends to prove by each specified item. A petition that fails to comply with the requirements shall be dismissed by the court unless remedied by the appellant. After a judgment in a criminal case has become conclusive there may be two more options left for the defendant: pardon, which is an executive privilege, and relief for substantive defects, which is an extraordinary court remedy. In the latter case relief may be granted for the benefit of the defendant if a member of the court, the prosecutor, or the defense counsel had incurred criminal liability that affected the sentence; if proof was forged or false testimony rendered; if new evidence might lead to acquittal or reduction in sentence; and, lastly, if the application of law to the case was obviously inconsistent with the governing legislative provision. If the application for relief is granted the Supreme Court may change the judgment immediately. Relief for grave procedural errors is also dealt with by the law; however, this hardly ever happens in practice.

THE COURTS OF JUSTICE

The homage paid to the lawspeakers and the courts in Viking society may have been mostly political rhetoric, such as the much quoted Icelandic adage: "The law shall be built on law and not by lawlessness laid waste. He who will not grant justice to others shall not himself enjoy the benefits of law." The saying is known in all the Nordic countries and may be a pertinent indication of how people looked at the machinery of law as a social stabilizer. Since the Vikings were cunning adapters when engaged in war and government in foreign countries, it is rather enigmatic that their countries of origin obdurately resisted the renaissance of the Roman notion of law and justice. A number of ecclesiastical and secular administrators, often men of Roman education, occasionally belonged to the entourage of the Nordic monarchs.

With time the courts of justice came to enjoy a high reputation in Swedish society. The judicial structure was modernized by importing the continental system of administrative tribunals. Montesquieu's ideas on the separation of governmental powers gained ground. King Gustavus II Adolphus in 1614 created the high court of appeal *(Svea Hovrätt)*, superimposed upon the local and provincial lawcourts. An administrative watchdog had existed since 1713, probably comparable to the Chinese Censorate *(Yuan)* and the Roman Censor. The Supreme Court *(Högsta domstolen)* was formed in 1789. To deal with juvenile delinquency Sweden in 1902 followed the Norwegian path to administrative action by children's welfare boards. In 1909 the Supreme Administrative Tribunal *(Regeringsrätten)* was established. Looking at the judicial system from the vantage point of the twentieth century it is probably fair to state that the Swedish courts have retained their distinct Nordic flavor. Where Swedish law had no answer, however, the court resorted to Roman law, thus sharing the general European legal tradition. Discussing case law in the seventeenth century, a scholar has stated: "The *Svea Hovrätt* often based its decisions directly on the Justinian legislation as it appears in the *Corpus Juris Civilis,* particularly when neither the indigenous Swedish law not the Romano-Germanic law offered any ready-made solution."[4]

With increased socioeconomic complexity subsequent to the industrial revolution and the rise of modern capitalism, the legislature adjusted cautiously. But with the emergence of social-democratic governments since 1932, law continued to be weighed more in favor of the collective, rather than accepting the American competitive, climate benefiting the individual. The Constitution is the principal guide for judges. The Swedish Instrument of Government was adopted in 1809 with a subsequent revision in 1974. It contains the basic human rights comparable to other modern democratic constitutions. To avoid legislative conflicts any new bill is subject to legal review by the Law Council *(lagrådet)* before the parliament is invited to act. Judges of the Supreme Court and the Supreme Administrative Tribunal participate in the deliberations of the Law Council. Judicial review as undertaken by the United States Supreme Court is not practiced by Swedish courts. Any legitimate grievances should be solved by means of the administrative tribunals or the Ombudsman. Compared with the Anglo-American judicature the role of precedents has a minor, though important, application as a rule for future guidance in analogous matters. The ambiguities particularly noticeable in United States criminal justice, with the contradictory orientations of goals and means, have been successfully bypassed in Sweden.

The National Law Code of 1734 is still in force even if much of its contents has been amended. The code established how the courts of law should be organized. The current authority on court organization is the Code of Judicial Procedure of 1942 which went into effect January 1, 1948. When the court machinery is activated fundamental principles govern the proceedings. The principle of orality means that the materials forming the basis of judicial decisions are to be presented orally, and directly to the decision-maker (the principle of immediacy). The principle of concentration implies that at a single proceeding or a series of closely related proceedings the court should pass judgment without delay. Perhaps the most important principle, at least when compared with the current American procedure, empowers the court to freely accept any material and seek out any source that might assist it in eliciting the truth: "Restraints on the evaluation of evidence imposed by formal proof rules were to be abolished. Instead, the court was to rely upon its own common sense and sound judgment in determining the relative importance which should be attributed to various items of proof."[5] The ancient tribal European principle that the questions of guilt should be left with a jury of honest and impartial free men has been modified in the Swedish judicial procedure. It will be discussed together with the composition of the court.

The judiciary is organized with a three-tier hierarchy of courts: the courts of first instance *(tingsrätter)*, the intermediate courts of appeal *(hovrätter)*, and the Supreme Court *(högsta domstolen)*. The more than hundred lower courts have different names in urban and rural areas, the former being called *rådhusrälter,* and the latter *häradsrätter*. Commonly, they are referred to as district courts. They vary greatly in size and play a dominant role in the judicial system. In principle there are no limitations on the jurisdiction of the district courts, regarding the subject areas of the cases. The legally trained judges serving in these courts are, broadly speaking, in a position of parity with the appeal court judges in respect to salary. According to the official view this provides part of the explanation why only about 5 percent of the total number of cases in the district courts pass to the courts of appeal. The president of a district court has the medieval title of *lagmann*. Working with him are one or more associate judges *(rådmän)* and a number of law graduates who complete the practical aspects of their career in this way. Instead of a trial by jury to decide on facts and a collegium of judges to settle matters of law, the district courts comprise the presiding judge, associate judges, and a panel *(nämnd)* of lay assessors. They all share in the determination of all factual and legal problems presented. In each court district there shall be eighteen lay judges or assessors according to Chapter 1, Section 5 of the code. A panel may normally include seven to nine persons; however, three, together with the professional judges, may constitute a quorum. The assessors are elected for six-year terms by local representative councils from the roster of eligible local citizens. Most of them are reelected for consecutive terms.

Since each lay assessor is on duty for at least ten days in any one year, the panels develop considerable experience over a period of time. The panel or *nämnd* serves mainly in cases concerning criminal offenses of a more serious nature and in family cases. In these cases the bench consists of a legally trained judge as chairman and five lay assessors. Having roots in medieval tradition the *nämnd* has constituted a significant element of democracy in Swedish public life. It should not be confused with the Anglo-American and Continental jury. Its members are concerned with points of fact, law, and the type of sanction to be imposed in criminal cases. A qualified majority of the lay assessors must agree in order to prevail over the contrary opinion of the judge. In practice such disagreements seldom occur. The Code provides for a special composition of the court in certain kinds of cases. The bench accordingly may include three professional judges or, in cases of minor importance, one such judge. In other types of cases the bench is composed of technical experts sitting alongside the legally trained judges. This occurs, for example, in cases concerning expropriation and real estate formation. Since over 95 percent of criminal and civil cases are adjudicated at the local level, the number of appeal courts *(hovrätter)* is currently limited to six. These are the courts of second instance, of which the most publicized has been the Svea Court of Appeal in Stockholm, established in 1614. The courts are composed of professional judges with no provision for lay assessors. Each court shall have a president, one or more division heads *(lagmän)* and associate judges *(hovrättsråd)*. Four judges constitute a quorum, but no more than five may sit in any one case. The courts of appeal supervise the lower courts within their circuits. Appeals against judgments of district courts can be carried without any restriction to a court of appeal. Decisions are reached by majority vote. The preparatory work is mainly done by junior judges undergoing training. Some of them later join the various ministries and administrative boards as legal secretaries.

The Supreme Court is the highest appellate court having jurisdiction over civil, criminal, and military cases. Technically, the decisions of the courts of appeal can be brought to the Supreme Court, but special permission from the court is necessary for the hearing of a case. In principle, only cases having an important bearing on the application of law will be heard. On the whole, only cases which are of interest from the point of view of possible precedents are tried before the Supreme Court. The screening of applications for review is conducted by a separate section of the court comprising three judges. They have the final word in accepting or rejecting judicial reviews. If permission is granted the case is heard by a bench of five justices constituting the quorum. As in the court of appeal decisions are reached by majority vote. The Court has a total of twenty-six judges working in three chambers and the Law Council. The preparatory work is performed by junior judges in the course of their training.

The Judicial Code has specified what qualifications are needed to become a judge. He shall be a Swedish citizen more than twenty-five years of age and shall have passed the tests of knowledge prescribed. The latter in practice means the completion of study at a university's law school. The professional judges at all levels are appointed by the executive government, i.e. the King in Council.

Under the Code there are no separate civil or criminal courts. But there are chapters dealing with court proceedings, generally in civil and criminal cases as they apply to the lower and intermediate courts, and in the Supreme Court. All court sessions are open to the public; however, minors may be denied admittance at the discretion of the presiding judge. He can also direct that hearings be held behind closed doors, e.g. in the interest of national security, industrial patent, or manufacturing secrets and during the disclosure of forensic psychiatric reports pertaining to the state of mind of defendants. The taking of photographs is prohibited during court hearings.

Minor offenses and misdemeanors subject to fines only are heard by a single judge of the district court. Offenses punishable by imprisonment for a maximum of one year or by dismissal from office are heard by a judge sitting with three lay assessors. Felonies are dealt with by a judge assisted by the full panel of lay assessors. The above applies to main hearings. A single judge administers preliminary and preparatory court hearings in civil cases. The Code also has specific rules to expedite a case in which there is substantial agreement as to the relevant factual and legal issues. In city courts three or four professional judges may be required for the trial of civil cases. To reiterate lower court procedures, proceedings in felony cases distinguish between the preliminary hearing and the trial. The police and the prosecutors are charged with the pretrial preparation. Civil proceedings are divided into the preparatory hearing and the main court session. In appellate cases the preparation, as well as the trial, is conducted by the officials of the court of appeal. Judges may call on probation officers to prepare reports on the personal situation of defendants, the purpose of which is to provide guidance for resocialization. Frequently also, the judge may require a profile of a defendant's mental state. This examination is conducted by a psychiatrist selected by the National Social Welfare Board. Psychiatric examinations on the average last less than four months.[6] In the case of offenders in custody, the country has three forensic psychiatric clinics for such examinations.

Sweden, like its Nordic neighbors, is painfully aware of the social and medical problems connected with the abuse of alcohol, narcotics, and drugs. Social welfare laws encourage the judges to use special care provisions for alcoholics, drug addicts, and mentally unstable persons. It may be suspected that a combination of these phenomena and suicidal tendencies has caused the sociomedical authorities to take these measures, bearing in mind the rather high suicide rate among the Swedish population.

Contrary to the trend in some countries including Denmark, the suppression of narcotics is vigorous. There is no motion to decriminalize the possession of use of marijuana. The severity of the problem has necessitated the assignment of a special prosecutor in the capital where an estimated 25 percent of schoolchildren have had contact with narcotics. The latter is a youth problem. This leads logically to the question of juvenile justice. The Nordic response to juvenile delinquency is a quasi-judicial body within the executive branch of local government. Persons below the age of fifteen who commit crimes cannot be sentenced to punishment. The competent authority is the Child Welfare Board. While police, in maintaining order and controlling crime in recent years, have been obliged to pay more attention to juvenile misbehavior, the measures that can be applied to this category are for the most part found in the Child Welfare Act of 1960.

Since World War II young persons have assumed a major share of the crime increase. Around 70 percent of the reported crimes can be traced to boys in the age group between fifteen and twenty-four. This is inversely proportional to their numbers in the total Swedish population. Here, as elsewhere in the Atlantic democracies, crime is generated by urbanization and population density. The administrative actions taken in connection with juvenile delinquency are in contrast to the judicial apparatus found in the United States, e.g. The Child Welfare Board is part of local government responsibilities and consists of five members: a minister (belonging to the Lutheran State Church), a public schoolteacher, at least two persons chosen for their dedication to the problems of children and youth, and usually one individual who is trained in law. The municipal council elects all members for a term of four years. The member is unpaid, although some expenditures are reimbursed. The more than 1,000 boards are functionally supervised by twenty-four administrative regions. The national coordination is managed by the Social Welfare Administration. Field work is performed by full-time salaried child welfare officers. In addition to their duties with juvenile offenders, they look after children born out of wedlock and, in some cases, children whose parents have separated. In conjunction with the report by a governmental commission on social affairs in 1974, the importance of close collaboration between child welfare boards, schools, and the police was emphasized. In trying to discover the needs of deviant minors and hopefully devise acceptable solutions, the board may enlist the services of psychiatric and psychological experts. In a big city an attempt to remedy the feeling of isolation among adolescents is made through institutionalized contact centers and motivation centers, that provide temporary accommodation, meals, work and health care, sheltered homes, and rehabilitation facilities. The latter two focus on adolescents with serious social, medical, and psychic problems—frequently alcohol and drug abusers. Realistically, the child welfare boards cannot always rely on persuasion and voluntary measures. The resident state prosecutor maintains close liaison with the boards concerning the disposition of serious delinquents. In conventional crime cases the prosecutor must consult with the board before deciding whether or not to waive prosecution. Pursuant to the Penal Code, Chapter 29, Section 1, a person who is not yet eighteen or who is twenty-one but not yet twenty-three years of age may be sentenced to youth imprisonment, if such sanction is deemed obviously more appropriate than another sanction. The sometimes questionable adequacy of measures may produce dissonance between the Prosecutor's Office and the board arising out of the different expectations of the two institutions. The prosecutor's decisions are normative and legalistic while the board members may be more concerned with the future consequences affecting the individual deviants. This fact is mainly inherent in the structures which have been summed up as follows:[7]

The Public Prosecutor's Office	*The Child Welfare Board*
1. A rather distinct goal	1. A rather vague goal
2. A state agency	2. A board elected by the legislative assembly of the municipality
3. Only state officials	
4. Officials placed in a hierarchial system making the decisions	3. Elected laymen — sometimes supplemented by a paid staff
5. The office situated at a middle level of the organization	4. A collegiate board making all important decisions
6. The office under strict control	5. The board part of a local self-government and also controlled by state authorities
7. The procedure rather formalized	6. The board controlled only in principle, not in detail
	7. The procedure rather informal

Actions by the boards largely resemble those of the juvenile courts. They can compel minors to spend time under supervision in special training schools and boarding homes. The philosophy is care and protection, not correctional punishment. Discussing social work with the maladjusted, a Swedish practitioner has made this observation:

Perhaps the main characteristic of Swedish social work is that it is directed towards helping not only clients with a good prognosis but also —and perhaps mostly—clients with bad prognosis. The ideal is respect for the individual's integrity and right of self-determination, avoiding at the same time neglects of clients who lack a real understanding of their situation and who therefore might not accept necessary treatment. This is why—according to current laws—the social welfare institutions in certain situations have at their disposal some means of coercion.[8]

Finally, it should be mentioned that even if persons are legally labelled youth they can be tried in the ordinary courts of law. The Child Welfare Board has no exclusive jurisdiction over minors, as the juvenile court has. Pretrial detention is sometimes justified in the interest of the common good. The principle of legality in Swedish criminal justice also imposes a duty on the state's attorney

The Structure of the Swedish System for Dealing with Juvenile Offenders

Authorities and Measures

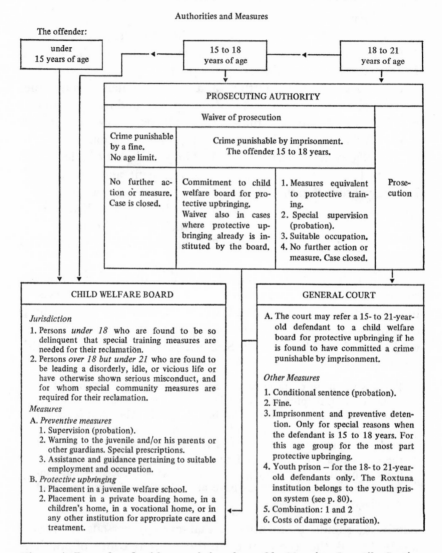

The offender:

| under 15 years of age | 15 to 18 years of age | 18 to 21 years of age |

PROSECUTING AUTHORITY

Waiver of prosecution

| Crime punishable by a fine. No age limit. | Crime punishable by imprisonment. The offender 15 to 18 years. | | Prosecution |

| No further action or measure. Case is closed. | Commitment to child welfare board for protective upbringing. Waiver also in cases where protective upbringing already is instituted by the board. | 1. Measures equivalent to protective training.
 2. Special supervision (probation).
 3. Suitable occupation.
 4. No further action or measure. Case closed. | |

CHILD WELFARE BOARD

Jurisdiction
1. Persons *under 18* who are found to be so delinquent that special training measures are needed for their reclamation.
2. Persons *over 18 but under 21* who are found to be leading a disorderly, idle, or vicious life or have otherwise shown serious misconduct, and for whom special community measures are required for their reclamation.

Measures
A. *Preventive measures*
 1. Supervision (probation).
 2. Warning to the juvenile and/or his parents or other guardians. Special prescriptions.
 3. Assistance and guidance pertaining to suitable employment and occupation.
B. *Protective upbringing*
 1. Placement in a juvenile welfare school.
 2. Placement in a private boarding home, in a children's home, in a vocational home, or in any other institution for appropriate care and treatment.

GENERAL COURT

A. The court may refer a 15- to 21-year-old defendant to a child welfare board for protective upbringing if he is found to have committed a crime punishable by imprisonment.

Other Measures
1. Conditional sentence (probation).
2. Fine.
3. Imprisonment and preventive detention. Only for special reasons when the defendant is 15 to 18 years. For this age group for the most part protective upbringing.
4. Youth prison — for the 18- to 21-year-old defendants only. The Roxtuna institution belongs to the youth prison system (see p. 80).
5. Combination: 1 and 2
6. Costs of damage (reparation).

Figure 4. Reproduced with permission from Ola Nyquist, *Juvenile Justice: A Comparative Study with Special Reference to the Swedish Child Welfare Board and the California Juvenile Court System* (London: MacMillan Company, 1960), p. 11.

to initiate public prosecution. When it comes to sentencing minors the law prohibits life imprisonment, and the court has the discretion to go below the minimum penalty prescribed in the particular status. Internment[9] or preventive detention applied to dangerous persistent criminals (psychopaths) is a protective measure in the interest of society. It is only used as an exceptional device for youths below the age of eighteen. Little purpose is served here to argue the pros and cons of the Child Welfare Board and the Juvenile Court. It is only pointed out that the former has attracted considerable interest in Anglo-American countries.

Since administration involves the exercise of power by the executive arm of government, administrative law is of constitutional and political importance, and separate courts have proved essential to review and interpret the administrative process in complex modern society. In Sweden the administrative tribunals are the most recent addition to the judiciary. A wide range of public policies are carried out by functional boards, e.g. in public safety, health, and education. These boards are not answerable to any individual cabinet minister. Only the king in council can reverse board decisions. There exists, therefore, a valid argument for a strong judicial control through the medium of administrative tribunals, of which there are several. The Government Court *(Regeringsrätten)* hears cases on law questions. The Chamber Court *(Kammarrätten)* deals with poor law cases and salary claims by civil servants. The Court of Social Insurance decides accident insurance cases, and the Labor Court settles disagreements pertaining to the interpretation of collective tariff agreements. The limited number of days lost in strikes can in part be attributed to the conciliatory role played by the latter.

To discourage secrecy in government, documents showing the decision-making process are accessible to the public. This is another safeguard against arbitrary administration. The use of administrative law as an instrument for guiding and controlling the bureaucracy has a firm tradition in Continental Europe. Judicial review embraces the extent of legal powers, the adequacy and fairness of the procedure, and the nature and scope of discretionary decisions. France has been the promoter of administrative justice. Napoleon in 1799 modernized the *Conseil d'Etat,* enabling it to make binding decisions. It is the competent court in which claims against the administration should be brought. The English attitude until 1947 has been: "The King can do no wrong," which now makes it possible to sue government departments. In the U.S.S.R. the Procuracy watches over administrative legality and encourages the exposure of bureaucratic abuses. The Swedish approach is closer to the French than to Anglo-American and Communist means of ensuring fairness. Article 18 of the Swedish Constitution of 1809 provides for the establishment of the Supreme Administrative Tribunal. Two thirds of its members shall have qualifications required for a judicial office. A general requirement is that the members have held civil office and manifested insight, experience, and honesty. Five members normally constitute the quorum when hearing cases of appeal from the subordinate administrative bodies. Conflicts of interest may occur. Police actions and discretionary decisions to some extent are part of the criminal justice process. Subsequently, it may sometimes be hard to decide whether complaints shall be heard by the regular or the administrative courts. In Sweden the institution of the ombudsman appears to have provided for an adequate solution.

A most fascinating aspect of the judiciary pertains to impeachment, that is, a criminal proceeding against a high public servant before a quasi-political court. Historically, it has always been a problem to harness the government elite. Again the presence of the Greco-Roman legacy is impressed upon one. Accusations that may be subject to impeachment have often been difficult to define and classify. The purpose often has been to remove influential politicians from the government arena by death, exile, or blinding. In Rome under a variety of pretenses, the *crimen laesae majestatis* or an offense against sovereignty was invariably invoked or instigated by the emperor. With the nineteenth century's era of constitutionalism, the power to impeach has shifted to the political parties through their elected representatives. The concept of high treason has usually been reserved for the political losers in war. Misconduct, malfeasance, or even crime in office are more in line with the contemporary happenings where political factions have demanded impeachment. The Ben Barka case in France and the American Watergate are characteristic. They were both crimes committed for political purposes in the vicinity of the head of state.

The authority for impeachment in Sweden is found in Articles

101 through 107 of the Constitution of 1809. The duty to initiate proceedings belongs to the ombudsmen and the attorney general. The court is to be presided over by the president of the Svea Court of Appeal and composed of the presidents of all the administrative boards of the kingdom. The composition to some extent depends on who is accused. To avoid details it is safe to state that high-ranking civil and military officers and judges are members.

The evolution of the democratic process in Sweden apparently has preserved the sociopolitical equilibrium because the Court of Impeachment *(Riksrätten)* has not been activated for over a century. In the wake of the February Revolution of France in 1848, riots and unrest were common in the Swedish cities. The Constitution Committee (Article 107) impeached cabinet ministers, none of whom were convicted. The last acquittal in 1854 convinced the politicians of the need for an electoral reform which came about in 1866. An impeachment of ministers proved more successful for the accusers in Norway, at that time united with Sweden under the same monarch. A judgment by the Court of Impeachment in 1884 enabled Norway to introduce a parliamentary political system thirty-three years before Sweden. The reduction of the king to a formal figurehead and the accountability of the cabinet to the legislature *(Riksdag)* has not necessitated impeachment or demands for it since.

FOOTNOTES

[1]F. Garraud in A. Esmein *A History of Continental Criminal Procedure* (1880) trans. in 1913 (South Hackensack: Rothman's Reprints, 1968) p. 3.

[2]A. Bruzelius and R. B. Ginsburg (Ed.) *The Swedish Code of Judicial Procedure* (South Hakensack: Fred B. Rothman & Company, 1968).

[3]*Ibid.* pp. 85 and 96.

[4]S. Jägerskiöld. "Roman Influence on Swedish Case Law in the 17th Century" in *Scandinavian Studies in Law* Vol. 2 (Stockholm: Almquist and Wiksell 1967), p. 1979.

[5]Bruzelius and Ginsburg, pp. 6-7.

[6]Nelson, p. 78.

[7]Britt-Mari Persson Blegvad. "A Case Study of Interorganizational Conflicts" in *Scandinavian Studies in Criminology*, Vol. 2, 1968, p. 28.

[8]Gunnel Swedner, *Social Work Practice and Social Work Professions in Sweden*, (Stockholm: Kumla Tryckeri, 1968), p. 73.

[9]In Swedish criminological usage internment is comparable with preventive detention in Anglo-Saxon systems.

CHAPTER 6

THE CORRECTIONAL ADMINISTRATION

The Law

O N JANUARY 1, 1965, a new Criminal Code went into effect. The new Criminal Code was founded on the concept of *prevention,* not *retribution.* The Code was also based on the precept that noninstitutional alternatives should be emphasized. This Code, which has replaced the former Penal Code of 1864, provides for the following main classes of sanctions:

1. the general punishments of fine and imprisonment;
2. punishment of crimes by public servants: suspension and removal from office, together with disciplinary measures against military men; and
3. other sanctions: conditional sentence, probation, youth prison, internment, and surrender to special care.

All sanctions are on an equal footing, and the selection of any one sanction is made solely with reference to the circumstances of a particular case.

Wherever possible, noninstitutional care is given preference to measures which deprive the offender of his liberty. This is a fundamental concept of the Swedish correctional system.

FINES: Except for drunkenness and disorderly conduct, all fines for designated offenses under the Criminal Code are imposed as day-fines *(dagsböter).* These are fixed numbers of days, ranging from a minimum of one to a maximum of 120 (rising as high as 180 if several crimes are punished concurrently). The system combines two elements: the amount of fine, determined by the offender's ability to pay, and the number of days, determined by the seriousness of the offense. Fines vary in amount from 48 cents to 120 dollars.

The court may convert unpaid fines to imprisonment ranging up to ninety days. Exception is made for nonpayment owing to financial difficulties, but an offender who deliberately seeks to evade his obligation must serve his term. Fines may also be imposed concurrently with certain other sanctions, such as conditional sentence, for one and the same offense.

IMPRISONMENT: Imprisonment is the Code's only liberty-depriving measure having a definite time span. It may be imposed for life or for a fixed period not shorter than one month or longer than ten years. A collective sentence for several crimes may be for as long as twelve years.

However, the time factor is essentially modified by the rules on parole. An inmate may be conditionally released after having served two-thirds, but no less than four months, of his sentence, provided he has behaved and shows promise of readaptation to society. Parole may also be considered after half the sentence is completed, but in that case the law stipulates that "compelling reasons" shall be present. The age of the offender or the imposition of a long prison term are recognized as two such reasons.

The parole system applies to an offender sentenced to life imprisonment as follows: If he has behaved well and can be expected to refrain from criminality in the future, he will have his sentence commuted to fourteen or fifteen years after having served about eight years of his term. He may qualify during the commuted term for parole under the rules given above.

Decisions on parole are taken by a supervisory board, which is automatically required to review cases well ahead of the qualifying date. But if the prison term in a particular case exceeds one year, the supervisory board shall formulate an opinion and refer the matter to a correctional board. The chief determinant of a decision on parole is the offender's "social prognosis." However, a parole will not be granted unless the offender has employment and satisfactory living quarters awaiting him on the outside. A decision on parole is accompanied by stipulation of a trial period equivalent to the remaining portion of the sentence, fixed in no case at less than one year. During this period the parolee is normally under supervision.

CONDITIONAL SENTENCE: Although conditional sentence is a

sanction in the technical sense, it may to all intents and purposes amount to conditional remission of another sanction. Conditional sentence may therefore be said to remit every sanction provided the offender does not commit a new crime for a trial period of two years. The sentence cannot be combined with supervision, nor can any conditions be affixed to it apart from the offender's obligation to pay damages.

Since a conditional sentence imposes very little in the way of restraint, eligibility is limited to persons with a more promising social prognosis, that is, to those deemed to be typical one-time offenders whose personal circumstances do not necessitate the support of society which supervision implies.

For purposes of ensuring general obedience to the law, it may sometimes be desirable to stiffen the punishment without thereby renouncing the grounds of individual deterrence which justify a conditional sentence. To deal with a case of this kind, the Criminal Code leaves scope for combining a conditional sentence with unconditional fines.

PROBATION AND PAROLE: Probation is thought of as a separate and independent sanction. Probation is considered *treatment* in an environment of freedom with or without supervision. In some cases probation may include treatment in an institution. This treatment normally takes place in one of four special institutions. These institutions are open and have special programs for evaluation and assistance from social workers, psychologists, and psychiatrists.

The role of approximately 250 probation-parole officers is that of an administrative supervisory relationship with the volunteer workers who actually handle the direct supervision of the probationer or parolee. Each volunteer will supervise one or two cases on a part-time basis. Approximately 12,000 volunteers supervise 23,000 probationers and parolees. The volunteer receives approximately twelve dollars per case per month.

In principle, probation may be classified with conditional sentence as a form of noninstitutional correction. But in view of various practical differences between the two, probation emerges as a considerably more serious type of restraint. Presentence investigations are ordered by the court and are normally carried out by a law clerk who is a lawyer under training for a judicial career.

While on probation, the offender may also be subject to approximately the same conditions as described above under conditional sentence.

An offender who violates the conditions of his probation runs the risk of forfeiting the court's verdict and having a more stringent sanction imposed upon him. The new sanction will be chosen with reference to what is considered most appropriate in the circumstances and will not be determined by the previous sentence.

Probation may also be combined with a brief stay at an institution. The length of this period, ranging from one to two months, is determined not by the court but by the supervisory board during the course of treatment, with regard to the requirement of each special case. The institutional stay, which is normally supposed to initiate enforcement of the sanction, is a resource available to the court to reinforce society's reaction against the crime. However, it should primarily be viewed as a means to break off the offender's criminal activity, remove him from an improper environment, and bring him under social and psychological observation as a possible basis for further treatment on the outside. As a rule, inside treatment is to be given at special institutions. Probated offenders under eighteen years of age may not be committed to an institution.

One of the legal grounds for probation is that it may not normally be prescribed if a minimum prison sentence of one year or more is stipulated for the particular crime. A person serving a prison term may be paroled when two thirds of his term has been completed. In special cases a person may be released after serving one half of the sentence but in no case until four months of the sentence have been served.

YOUTH PRISON: Youth prison is a liberty-depriving sanction primarily intended for the 18-to-21 age group. Under the Criminal Code a court may impose it on offenders under eighteen, but only to a limited extent and then mostly with respect to young persons who may be considered to belong to the older than eighteen group by virtue of their physical and mental development. In exceptional cases offenders under eighteen or between twenty-one and twenty-three years of age may be sentenced to youth prison.

The Criminal Code further adds that this sanction may be imposed if the direction and training which youth imprisonment is meant to give are deemed appropriate in view of the youth's personal development, conduct, and other circumstances. It follows from this stipulation that youth imprisonment would not be indicated unless a longer period of institutional care is needed to resocialize the offender. Nor may this sanction be considered when deprivation of liberty is principally justified on grounds of general crime deterrence.

As a condition for imposing youth imprisonment, the crime must be serious enough to be punished by imprisonment in the first place. This rules out violations of the law which are punishable by fines alone. If the crime is heinous, however, the court may see fit in many cases to impose a sanction of imprisonment.

In the words of the Code, the treatment of one sentenced to youth imprisonment is to take place "within and outside an institution." The treatment may last for a maximum of five years, of which not more than three are in an institution. As a rule a youth may not be transferred to care outside the institution until one year has passed, after which he must submit to at least two years of noninstitutional care, making a minimum total of three years. The point here is that length of treatment is not fixed by the court but is determined during the course of treatment.

Decisions on transfer to care outside an institution are rendered by a national body, the Youth Correctional Board. During the period of treatment outside the institution, the youth shall be under supervision. He may also be required to abide by various restrictions of the same kind as those noted for conditional sentence.

INTERNMENT: As defined by the Code, internment is a long-lasting deprivation of liberty the duration of which is not fixed in advance. It is intended for dangerous recidivists who are not deemed receptive to other corrective measures.

A sentence to internment may be imposed if the crime is punishable by imprisonment for at least two years and if the court finds, regarding the offender's mental condition, conduct and other circumstances that necessitate prolonged and indefinite incarceration to prevent further serious criminality on his part.

The indefiniteness of internment lies in the absence of a specified date for release. What the court does instead is to fix a given minimum term of at least one year and at most twelve years for institutional treatment. When the minimum period expires, it then becomes the responsibility of the Internment Board to decide whether the internee is ready for the outside treatment which the Code stipulates as a compulsory follow-up of institutional care. If the Internment Board rules against an internee the first time, it must regularly reconsider the question of his transfer to outside care. However, the internee may not be kept in custody for longer than five years after expiration of the minimum period without court consent. The court may then order the extension of institutional care for three years at a time.

With respect to outside care, the offender shall be under supervision. At the discretion of the board, supervision over an internee under outside care is terminated after an uninterrupted period of three years.

SURRENDER TO SPECIAL CARE: This chapter of the Code contains a number of sanctions whose element of kinship is that their details are spelled out by other pieces of social legislation: the Child Welfare Act, the Temperance Act, and the Mental Health Act.

A. If a court decides that the remedies available under the correctional system are inadequate in a particular case and that better alternatives are offered under the Child Welfare Act, it may turn over the offender to a local child welfare committee. It is assumed here, of course, that the case comes under the purview of the Act by virtue of the offender's being under twenty-one.

B. If a court established a need for special care due to the abuse of alcoholic beverages by the offender, it may surrender him for such care under the Temperance Act. Before doing so, however, the court must hear the local temperance board. A restriction on the use of this sanction is that it may be imposed only with respect to relatively minor crimes.

C. Surrender for special care under the Mental Health Act involves commitment to a mental hospital, subject to a recommendation to this effect by the medical profession. In principle, a decision to commit the offender to a mental hospital must be made solely with reference to the situation prevailing at the time of the court's verdict.

D. An additional sanction, aimed exclusively at mentally abnormal offenders, is surrender for open psychiatric care. However, the abnormality must be of a nature responsive to adequate treatment outside a mental hospital. A further condition is that the gravity of the crime does not necessitate greater restraint for the protection of society.

YOUNG OFFENDERS: In Sweden the age of criminal responsibility is fixed at fifteen. Offenders under this age do not come under the jurisdiction of the courts but are the responsibility of the child welfare committee. An offender who is already fifteen when he commits his crime may in principle be brought before a court and sentenced under the Criminal Code.

The age group from fifteen to seventeen years, inclusive, has long occupied a special position in Swedish jurisprudence, marked by constraint in the use of correctional measures which deprive offenders of their liberty. This attitude is underscored in the Criminal Code, which in principle holds that responsibility for offenders in the group falls outside the jurisdiction of the courts. Most offenders in this group are accordingly surrendered to the child welfare committee. This is done in either of two ways: The public prosecutor may decide to dismiss the indictment; or the court, after trying the case, may order surrender of the young defendant for care under the Child Welfare Act.

Persons in the 18-to-20 age group may also be surrendered for care under the Child Welfare Act, even though the correctional system is primarily responsible for the treatment of offenders after they reach their 18th birthday.

The child welfare committee relies primarily on measures of a preventive nature, consisting of cautioning, supervision, and different types of supportive measures. If these are deemed to be ineffective, however, the committee may decide to take the young offender into custody for social therapy. He is then either put in a private home, boarding school, or the like or committed to an approved school.

While the Criminal Code was in the process of formulation

prior to 1965, there was considerable discussion of the question: Should fifteen- to seventeen-year-olds be sentenced to imprisonment and, if so, to what extent? The original draft excluded the imprisonment sanction altogether. But as is evident from the foregoing account, the final version of the law was not so categorical.

The applicability of youth imprisonment to offenders under eighteen has been described above. Concerning the other sanctions, internment is ruled out in practice for this age group, and the Code makes no special provision for fifteen- to seventeen-year-olds with respect to the sanctions summarized under "Surrender to Special Care" earlier in this chapter. The latter sanctions, however, are applied to this age group only in very exceptional cases.

In principle, care at an approved school runs for an indefinite period. But if a pupil is eighteen years old at the time of admission, he shall be discharged not later than his twenty-first birthday. A similar maximum of three years is observed in practice for older pupils. The following actions can be taken against young offenders who for various reasons are deemed unsuitable for care under the Child Welfare Act.

The public prosecutor is entitled to dismiss the indictment against fifteen- to seventeen-year-olds if the particular circumstances of a case so warrant. But unless the offense is trivial, the decision to waive prosecution is made under the assumption that the case will be turned over to a child welfare committee for appropriate action. In cases where the prosecutor thinks it better to press the indictment, even though the offense is minor and therefore does not require more restraining measures, the usual sanction is to impose fines.

Regarding the applicability of conditional sentence or probation to the youngest offenders, the general rule is to subordinate these sanctions to treatment under the Child Welfare Act. But if special reasons to arrange for open care under the correctional system exist in exceptional cases, the supervision required for probation makes this sanction preferable to a conditional sentence, which to all intents and purposes amounts to a waiver of prosecution. It is assumed that such probation will not be accompanied by commitment to an institution.

The correctional system is allowed broader scope in dealing

with offenders in the 18-to-21 age group. Thus, the courts are empowered to impose not only fines but also conditional sentence and probation, both institutional and noninstitutional, with no restrictions. However, use of the imprisonment sanction is still limited, though there are fewer restrictions as compared with those for the youngest category of offenders. If deprivation of liberty for not too short a period is considered necessary, the court may sentence the offender to youth prison. (See Appendix A for a description of the Swedish Association for Penal Reform.)

NATIONAL CORRECTIONAL ADMINISTRATION

The management of Sweden's correctional system, both in its institutional and noninstitutional forms, is exercised by the National Correctional Administration, an autonomous authority subordinate to the Ministry of Justice. With a staff of about 320, the administration is headed by a director-general and consists of two main departments: treatment and security, and work and education.

The division of headquarters are served by three bodies collectively known as the central boards: the Correctional Board, the Youth Correctional Board, and the Internment Board. Though the boards are administratively separate from the National Correctional Administration, there is some overlapping of personnel in that the administration's director-general or his alternate is also a member of these boards. Each board has five members with a high-ranking judge as the presiding officer.

The Correctional Board functions as an appellate body in relation to the supervisory boards and is vested with the authority to review certain of their decisions. Review is mostly concerned with the granting of paroles, as well as with certain other measures and regulations which a supervisory board may have decided with respect to a parolee, e.g. designation of the area in which he is permitted to move or of his employment, or a decision to prolong or revoke the parole.

The most important task of the Youth Correctional Board is to decide, within the time limits specified by the Criminal Code, on the transfer of youth-prison inmates to noninstitutional care or on terminating the sanction completely. To some extent, as defined in the Criminal Code, the Board also performs an appellate function since it reviews decisions by supervisory boards relating to inmates of youth prisons.

Lastly, the status of the Internment Board, *vis-à-vis* internees, corresponds in essentials with that of the Youth Correctional Board in relation to its clientele. However, it has the special duty, when requested, of informing a court whether or not it considers internment to be an appropriate sanction. For purposes of institutional classification Sweden consists of correctional groups, divided on both a regional and functional basis. The regional groups are five in number: Northern, Eastern, Western, Southern, and Inland, all intended for male offenders sentenced to fixed terms of imprisonment. There are three functional groups called special groups: (1) The institutions of the Security Group are for male internees. (2) The Youth Group deals primarily with male inmates of youth prisons and secondarily with young men sentenced to imprisonment. (3) Female offenders, regardless of the sanction imposed on them, are assigned to the Women's Group. Each group has its own superintendent, who in effect acts as regional representative of the National Correctional Administration.

When the Criminal Code went into effect, the two main forms of care were coordinated by inserting all protective officer districts into the five regional correctional groups. This was intended to emphasize their interrelationship and, at the same time, to make their administration effective and smooth-working. In regard to the care and treatment of their charges, officials in the noninstitutional sector are immediately accountable to the supervisory board concerned.

INSTITUTIONAL CARE

A correctional group consists of a central institution and a number of auxiliary institutions. The central institution is usually the largest within a group and is always the closed or security type. In addition to the regular custodial quarters, it contains various special wards for treatment of the mentally and physically ill, and for isolation, reception, intractable inmates, etc.

The auxiliary institutions are of different types and include both closed and open units of varying capacity. One of the larger closed auxiliaries is Tidaholm in the Western Group with 230 places, which came into use at the end of the 1950's. Most of the auxiliaries, however, have much smaller accommodation.

Certain closed institutions are jails for offenders awaiting trial. Until such time as additional jails become available, however, most of the offenders thus remanded are assigned to a specially reserved ward of a closed institution for normal prison clientele.

The open institutions are also diverse in character. A significant innovative institution is Tillberga in the Eastern Group, where all 120 inmates are employed in workshops which are fully comparable with the most modern civilian facilities in terms of design and equipment. Most of the open auxiliary institutions, however, command small resources and are, moreover, of very limited capacity. Since January 1, 1965 the correctional system has included a new type of open facility known as probation institutions. They are intended for clientele sentenced to short-term institutional treatment as part of the probation sanction. Another class of open institution consists of the "pre-release homes," where offenders spend the final months of their institutional treatment. During this time they work on the open market for pay at regular union scales but are required to spend their leisure time in the home.

Once the offender comes under the purview of the National Correctional Administration, the criterion of allocation, in regard to an unarrested offender, is to place him in a suitable correctional group. Assignment to any of the five regional groups is primarily made with reference to the offender's actual place of residence. Consideration may also be given to other factors, for instance, the existence of a special ward where suitable treatment can be provided. The specific choice of institution within a group is left with the group superintendent.

With regard to arrested offenders sentenced to punishment of fixed duration, they are normally placed within the group where the jail is located. Persons sentenced to youth imprisonment and internment are automatically assigned to the Youth and Security Groups, respectively. Female offenders are placed within the

Women's Group.

At the level of the group superintendent, assignment is made with particular regard for the treatment investigation. Since this investigation usually takes place at a central institution, the inmate spends his initial period of confinement there. The preliminary placement of short-term offenders, who by definition do not undergo treatment investigation, is made with reference to their case history or other available documentation. They are generally committed directly to a suitable auxiliary institution.

Generally, offenders are not systematically differentiated in the sense that every institution is reserved for a specific type of clientele. Instead, the general rule is for an institution to admit offenders of different categories regardless of their crime, length of sentence, previous criminal record, and other similar circumstances. The differentiation that is made, nevertheless, in the choice between closed or open facilities is based on such factors as the offender's reliability and conduct in disciplinary terms, the existence of a special ward, or the like.

Some smaller institutions of the open type are set aside for clientele having no previous criminal record. In a number of cases open establishments have been earmarked for typical short-term offenders such as drunken drivers and objectors to military service.

Inmates with an aptitude for scholastic studies are eligible for admission to a small open institution at Uppsala, which enables enrolees to devote themselves full time to their education, naturally in observance of necessary restrictions and guidance.

All new inmates are initially assigned to the institution at Uppsala, which serves as a reception and classification center. For a period generally ranging from one to two months, they undergo the customary treatment investigation and also take a theoretical and practical aptitude test, the latter administered in the institution's general workshop. The knowledge of individual abilities thus provided forms the basis of assignment to the other institutions, with particular consideration being given to the inmates' vocational aptitudes, mentality and intellectual level, and reliability.

As a matter of course, clientele may also be differentiated within an institution. This is particularly true of the larger institutions equipped with various special wards and of the Hinseberg institution for women, where the many categories of inmates necessitate carefully considered assignment to different departments.

WORK PROGRAMS: Institutional care subscribes to the policy of full employment. Every able-bodied inmate who can work a normal 42-hour week is made to do so. The sole exceptions are made for offenders pending trial and for the ill or disabled. For a total potential institutional population of 6,000, about 4,000 openings are available in industry and another 1,000 in farming and forestry. The remaining clientele are put to simpler tasks in cells (offenders pending trial who wish to work) or to kitchen and maintenance duties.

The workshops at the new institutions are fully comparable in every respect with their counterparts in civilian life. Even the older institutions do their utmost to organize their work programs in accordance with present-day manufacturing principles.

Emphasis in the manufacturing sector is on iron and steel products, woodworking, and the production of clothing. Some institutions specialize in plastics, while others run large-scale laundries and a few even have their own printing plants. Building and construction comprise another important industry, having grown rapidly in the past few years and offering every promise of further expansion; institutional manpower has so far been engaged in the construction of several open institutions, but there are plans to assign it to other types of building as well. All work is remunerated, with piece rates used wherever possible. Average earnings come to about fifteen dollars per week and are equally divided into disposable income and savings. The inmate is free to spend the former; the savings are accumulated until release, but permission may be granted to draw on them for other purposes if the special case so warrants. The market value of all goods and services produced amounted to about $20 million in the 1969-1970 fiscal year.

An experiment to pay inmates at open-market rates is being conducted at Tillberga (see Appendices B and C), the new "factory prison" which makes a specialty of prefabricated timber houses. In return, the inmates will be required to pay taxes and buy their own food.

EDUCATION AND VOCATIONAL TRAINING: Apart from the performance of regular work, the inmates are more frequently allowed to take theoretical or practical vocational training. In addition to the institution at Uppsala, the institution at Härnösand offers full-time courses at the secondary school level. Some institutions cooperate with nearby folk high schools, where teachers hold daily classes at the institutions for academically oriented inmates. Other institutions have separate departments for inmates who take correspondence courses, in which they receive help from tutors.

Within the youth sector, emphasis is put on vocational training combined with general education subjects. To keep pace with the ever growing importance that vocational training has assumed for adults in the large society, the institutions have provided greater opportunities in this field for their adult clientele.

FURLOUGH: Permission to be absent from institutions was first granted on an official basis at the of the 1930's. Since then the system of furloughs has been developed to make it a recurrent and essential element of institutional care.

Furloughs fall into two classes, special and regular. The chief purpose of a special furlough is to enable an inmate to visit a seriously ill relative or to attend the funeral of a member of his family. Among the other approved purposes is job-hunting in advance of imminent release. It is also common to let an inmate travel on his own when being transferred from one institution to another (transportation furlough).

The regular furloughs are meant to combat the negative consequences that undeniably follow from a period of incarceration. Such a furlough helps the offender to maintain ties with his family and with a normal life on the outside. The regular furloughs vary in duration according to the circumstances. Thus, the qualification period for the first furlough depends on the term of imprisonment, whether the term is served in an open or closed institution, and the nature of the punishment. To take an example, a youth-prison pupil already receives his first furlough after three months, while a person sentenced to imprisonment for life must wait two years. There is a two-month interval between the regular furloughs.

Youth-prison pupils qualify for the initial furlough after three months, with subsequent furloughs grantable every third month.

Internees are bound by rules which essentially conform with those governing at closed institutions for inmates sentenced to imprisonment. Initial furloughs are usually for forty-eight hours plus travel time, increasing to seventy-two hours for subsequent furloughs.

In 1970 a total of 14,270 furloughs were granted. There were 1,261 (9%) failures to return and 571 (4%) other violations, such as late return or nonavoidance of intoxicating liquors.

EXPERIMENTS WITH TREATMENT METHODS: For the past few years long-term inmates have been afforded the opportunity to spend several summer weeks with close relatives at a special institution under vacation-like conditions. One institution runs three family dwellings which are available to inmates serving long sentences who wish to live together with their families. This experiment has turned out extremely well.

To facilitate visits by relatives the institution at Ulriksfors (Northern Group) has established a visiting hotel. The visitor can rent a room here at cost and spend a weekend together with the inmate.

NONINSTITUTIONAL CARE

Noninstitutional care is intended not only for previous inmates but also for those sentenced to probation, whether or not it is connected with institutional treatment. The system of noninstitutional care is structured with reference to the supervisory boards and the protective officer organization.

Management and inspection of the extramural correctional system are vested in the forty-seven supervisory boards by the Criminal Code. These are autonomous bodies and as such are not subject to the authority of the National Correctional Administration. Every board normally consists of five members with the chairman versed in the law. Matters concerning inmates are presented before the institutional wardens or their assistant. Matters relating to noninstitutional care are presented for consideration by a protective officer or his assistant. Among the duties of the supervisory boards are to appoint supervisors, to impose conditions on offenders, and to take action in cases of violations.

Fieldwork in this sector is the responsibility of the protective officer organization, and there are forty-two districts for this purpose. Four of them are special districts intended for special categories of clientele, i.e. internees or young offenders.

Substantial additions have been made to staff in recent years for various reasons, such as to enable protective officers and their assistant to take over more of the supervisory burden in the more serious cases. Even so, the operation of noninstitutional care on the desired scale will have to depend on the availability of voluntary supervisors. A numerical comparison brings out this point clearly: There are almost 12,000 volunteers working in noninstitutional care, while the personnel plan of the protective officer organization provides for only about 325 positions—a figure that includes clerical staff.

Laymen comprise a large proportion of the voluntary supervisors. Thus, a parolee or probationer may be looked after by a friend of his at the workplace, a teacher, or a youth leader. The supervisor is the one to whom his charge shall turn first of all for advice and support, both in purely personal, as well as financial, matters. Voluntary supervisors receive no more than nominal pay for their work, amounting to twelve dollars per month for each case under supervision.

CHAPTER 7

CONCLUSION

SOCIAL CONTROL or social defense encompasses a variety of phenomena in modern society. Traditionally, penal law has taken care of crime control while police legislation or regulatory law deals with public safety, health, and welfare. The term *criminal justice* today denotes an important government function.

The idea that institutions dealing with various aspects of criminal justice should be perceived as an integrated system belongs to the twentieth century. In the United States the various reports by the President's Commission on Law Enforcement and Administration of Justice (1967) advocate this line. The processing of criminals seems to fit the dynamics of a system's approach since the historical master pattern has shifted from retribution and compensation, prevention, and deterrence to treatment and rehabilitation. Insight can be gained and improvements made by treating the organizations and their operations as a system, rather than as independent units with separate functions, personnel, and clientele, i.e. as a nonsystem.

Sweden has pursued a system's approach to criminal justice with various reforms since 1965 that have affected components concerned with the problems of law violations.

History abounds with examples of barbarous means by which sociopolitical control has been achieved, Stalin's and Hitler's genocides being the recent extremes. The democratic alternative ought to be the application of moderate, proportionate means of maintaining and restoring orderly relations. But the domestic problem cannot be viewed in isolation. There are crucial external factors over which small countries have little control.

The English historian, Sir John R. Seeley (1834-1895), once asserted that the degree of internal freedom in a country is inversely proportional to the political and military pressure on its frontiers. This observation seems totally overlooked by the con-

118

temporary compatriot and writer, Roland Huntford, who has described the Swedes as "the new totalitarians." If Sir John's assertion is correct, it is apparent that none of the Nordic countries can afford the luxury of high risk and high reward that has been accompanied in other countries by an increasing degree of predatory behavior and subsequent victimization. In spite of meager natural resources and small populations, the Nordic countries appear to have retained a high level of domestic peace and order following the painful adaptation during the Industrial Revolution. Among them Sweden has been the dominant promoter of planned change by creating strong institutions. It can be readily observed that the socioeconomic progress has occurred in a homogeneous and cohesive society. Aspects of the social structure, according to an American sociologist, exert pressure upon individuals which may result in delinquency.[1] This pressure is mainly related to imperfect acculturation. Integration means the setting of acceptable goals, as well as the ability of the out-groups to internalize the accepted means for obtaining the goals. Anomie and alienation account for much criminal conduct. A look at other societies with greater resources may confirm that the introduction of value-conflicts through immigration tends to cause partial, though serious, breakdown of the social fabric if the out-groups are not assimilated and integrated into society. If the experience in some other countries may be used for comparative purposes it is safe to predict that should a situation with competing cultures take place in the Nordic countries the relative social peace would be gone.

When people feel compelled to move into walled and privately guarded communities and retain firearms for self-defense, societal cohesion suffers. If everyone's safety depends on his ability to defend himself, there is anarchy.[2]

The sociopolitical equilibrium in Sweden discounts both the notions of totalitarianism and of anarchy. The rewards have been sufficient to firmly maintain the allegiance of the population to the existing political system.

Can the controversial concept of *national character* elucidate the Swedish paradox? Some may question the inclination to make commonsense distinctions between the life-style, attitude, and appearance of people from different countries.

However, one may indeed be able to list and measure demographic and institutional qualities, assessing their similarities and dissimilarities for the purpose of discovering the extent of consensus about need satisfaction. With regard to the perception of criminal justice, a partial answer has been attempted in the preceeding pages.

It is probably too ambitious to give equal credit to the Swedish police force in terms of its impact on human behavior as an anthropologist has claimed for the English police.[3] Reference is made to the emphasis on prevention of aggression, on police officers preserving the peace by demonstrating the characteristic bobby's (policeman's) self-restraint. The qualities of self-discipline, sensitivity, fairness, and impartiality, exercised in a climate of lower-class violence, have resulted in a profound modification of the character of the urban population over a period of some 150 years in England.

Swedish society emerging from peasantry never adopted feudalism and the subsequent rigid stratification of the population as in England. There were stronger egalitarian forces in Sweden, encouraging solidarity and law-abiding attitudes. The trustworthiness of the Swedish police can be described as being inversely proportional to their influence.

Cross-culturally, the distinction is even more pronounced. When Doctor Grassberger of Austria and Doctor Kinberg of Sweden, two leading criminologists, visited the United States in the 1930's they found the American attitude toward law different from European traditions. The legislature and the judiciary grind in America as they do in Europe, but the average American cares little what comes out of it.

But is Sweden the "ray of sun" as some newspaper reporters perceive it? Frequent arguments in the West are connected with the stigma of socialism and the elimination of private enterprise. Yet an English business reporter recently stated: "Sweden's left-wing Social-Democratic Premier, Olof Palme, has less of the economy in his hands than did Edward Heath's Tory Government in Britain, even before Tony Benn's onward surge. Less than 10 percent of Swedish gross national product is accounted for by State enterprise."[4]

When the slogans are dismissed and the realities squarely faced, what emerges can be expressed like this: "In an era of revolutionary upheaval, Sweden stands as an exemplary model of progressive sociopolitical transformation. Since the beginning of the century Sweden has succeeded in combining rapid industrialization with the attainment of an effective pluralist democracy. . . . One of the world's most advanced and stable nations, Sweden illustrates important common feature of modernity."[5]

It is doubtful whether this can be accomplished without wholehearted mobilization, shown by a high degree of political participation. This involvement is not limited to a high turnout at elections. Participatory management in private companies by members of the labor force, as well as lay judges; a lay element on probation boards and local police councils; and political representatives on the policy-making boards of the national administrative agencies reinforce the perception of Sweden as a firm democratic bastion. (See Figure 5 which describes the organization of criminal justice in Sweden.) Evidently, this participatory role could not have succeeded without a motivational attitude that sets a high value on deliberate voluntary efforts.

National policies are generally thought of as determining factors in a country during a period in which global interaction and interdependence have been clearly recognizable. A blend of factors has brought the Nordic nations together. The aggressive designs revealed by two major powers during World War II caused the collapse of the Baltic states and reduced Finland. Three of the Nordic countries now have common territorial land or water boundaries with a totalitarian superstate (Russia). Responsible government must convince a people that the necessity of survival depends on the distance from the potential threat. Currently, it may be hard to predict whether an external threat in the north is potentially real or fancied.

Nevertheless, Nordic integration has become a realistic goal, even if the attempts to form a defense union have failed. The visible accomplishments of integration have been sympathetically and expertly discussed by an American historian:

These five Nordic states—Denmark, Finland, Iceland, Norway, and Sweden—have lived in amity with each other for a century and a half

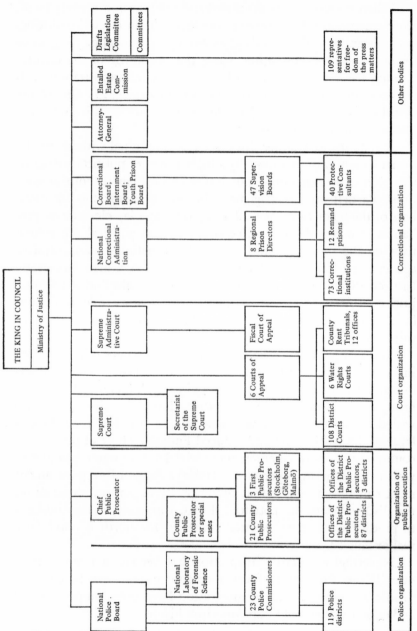

Figure 5. Organization of criminal justice in Sweden.

and have sought during the twentieth century to create a community which will maintain peace among themselves and with other nations. They have constructed institutions to implement this northern peace and have shown a common front so often that other nations usually regard the north of Europe as comprising an integrated area.[6]

The Nordic Council, formed in 1952, *inter alia* has been engaged in legislative coordination and criminological research.

Occasionally the argument is heard that the codification of law exemplified by criminal and procedural codes tends to rigidify the institutional framework, as contrasted to the flexibility allegedly existing in common law countries. However, when much emphasis is placed on teaching the actors in criminal justice the interpretation, enforcement, and application of the principles underlying the specific criminal and procedural statutes, discretionary fairness is facilitated, and less importance is attached to arrest.

It is acknowledged that the broad guidelines offered by the Swedish Code of Judicial Procedure lean in favor of community safety rather than protecting criminal suspects. Subsequently, case law with a highly technical and legalistic approach to crime control is avoided.

As to the potential for adjusting to change an Australian scholar has stated:

> The Swedes, like the English, have a gift for transforming institutions by a course of usage, and the Ombudsman has been so transformed. . . .
> The transformation of the Ombudsman into the people's guardian against the government has been accelerated by the fact that Sweden was among the earliest of the parliamentary democracies to adopt in a wholehearted way the Welfare State and extensive planning, with the accompanying danger of bureaucratic disregard for individual liberties.[7]

The authors wish to present the following assumptions as a final commentary to the description of criminal justice in Sweden:

1. Sweden's geopolitical location and philosophy maintain a higher level of obedience to traditional mores and law.
2. A planned international sociopolitical process within the Nordic countries (Denmark, Finland, Iceland, Norway, and Sweden) is fostering a higher level of integration, i.e. criminal justice cooperation.
3. To accomplish conformity to criminal law Sweden uses the

ancient continental philosophy, influenced by Roman law and pre-Napoleonic law, which leaves adjudication of certain crimes with the executive (police or prosecutor), while more serious crimes are dealt with by the court. Consent by the defendants must be obtained in all cases for executive action; otherwise, the case will automatically be dealt with by the court, regardless of the seriousness of the crime.

4. The correctional approach copes with rehabilitation by stressing the socialization process, i.e. movement away from large institutions to smaller community-based facilities which would facilitate inmate-family interaction, conjugal visitation, halfway houses, and economic integration with market wages paid to the inmate for motivated employment. A unified probation-parole system emphasizes policymaking by the lay public represented by trade unions, employer associations, and politicians. Correctional experts, e.g. psychiatrists, psychologists, sociologists, and lawyers, are utilized for advice only, not for making policy or decisions.

FOOTNOTES

[1]Robert K. Merton, *Social Theory and Social Structure* (New York: The Free Press of Glencoe, 1949), pp. 125-149.

[2]Ramsey Clark, *Crime in America* (New York: Simon & Schuster, 1970), p. 88.

[3]Geoffrey Gorer, *Exploring English Character* (New York: Criterion Books, 1955), pp. 305-311.

[4]Colin Chapman. "Sir Don's Swedish Model" in *The Observer*, London, January 12, 1975.

[5]M. Donald Hancock, *Sweden: The Politics of Post-Industrial Change* (Hinsdale: The Dryden Press, 1972), p. 1.

[6]Raymond E. Lindgren, *Norway—Sweden: Union, Disunion and Scandinavian Integration* (Princeton: Princeton University Press, 1959), p. 3.

[7]Geoffrey Sawer, *Ombudsmen* (Melbourne: Melbourne Universiyt Press, 1964), p. 8.

A BRIEF BIBLIOGRAPHY

Anderson, S. V. *The Nordic Council*. Seattle: University of Washington Press, 1967.

Andrén, N. B. I. *Modern Swedish Government*. Stockholm: Almqvist & Wicksell, 1968.

Becker, H. K. *Police Systems of Europe*. Springfield, Illinois: Thomas, 1973.

Fact Sheets on Sweden. Up-to-date information issued periodically by The Swedish Institute, Stockholm.

Hancock, D. M. *The Politics of Post-Industrial Change*. Hinsdale, Illinois: The Dryden Press, 1972.

Hjellemo, E. O. and H. K. Becker. "Sweden 1974: A Comparative Experience in Criminal Justice," *Journal of California Law Enforcement*, Vol. 9, No. 3, January, 1975.

Huntford, R. *The New Totalitarians*. New York: Stein & Day, 1972.

Nelson, A. *Responses to Crime: An Introduction to Swedish Criminal Law and Administration*. New Jersey, Fred B. Rothman, 1972.

Nyquist, O. *Juvenile Justice: A Comparative Study with Special Reference to the Swedish Child Welfare Board and the California Juvenile Court Systems*. London: MacMillan, 1969.

Oakley, S. *A Short History of Sweden*. New York: Praeger, 1966.

Orfield, L. B. *The Growth of Scandinavian Law*. Philadelphia: Temple University Press, 1953.

Rowat, D. C. *The Ombudsman: Citizen's Defender*. London: Allen & Unwin, 1965.

Rustow, D. A. *The Politics of Compromise: A Study of Parties and Cabinet Government in Sweden*. New Jersey: Princeton University Press, 1955.

Samuelson, K. *From Great Power to Welfare State: 300 Years of Swedish Social Development*. London: Allen & Unwin, 1968.

Scandinavian Studies in Criminology. Annual issues beginning 1965. Oslo University Press (and London: Tavistock).

Scobbie, I. *Sweden (Nation of the Modern World Series)*. New York: Praeger, 1972.

The Penal Code of Sweden (transl. Thorsten Sellin). Stockholm: Ministry of Justice, 1965.

The Swedish Code of Judicial Procedure (Transl. A. Bruzelius & R. Ginsburg). New Jersey: Fred B. Rothman. 1968.

Tomasson, R. F. *Sweden: Prototype of Modern Society*. New York: Random House, 1970.

Weeks, K. M. *Ombudsman Around the World: A Comparative Chart*. Berkeley: Institute of Governmental Studies, 1973.

APPENDIX A

NATIONAL SWEDISH ASSOCIATION FOR PENAL REFORM (KRUM)*

Objectives

K RUM SEEKS TO DISSECT and combat the class society which, owing to its unequal distribution of power and wealth, promotes the formation of groups who are socially, economically, and culturally disadvantaged.

KRUM seeks to abolish imprisonment and other coercive deprivations of liberty in the correctional system, child and youth welfare, mental health services, care of alcoholics, drug addicts, disabled persons, etc.

KRUM wants to put crime, the punishment of crime, and the correctional system in a broader picture. The causes of crime should be sought not in individual frailties but in social evils. KRUM questions the merits of a society which creates disadvantaged groups and almost exclusively permits members of these groups to bear the brunt of criminal punishment.

KRUM also questions and rejects all the arguments that are usually advanced to defend deprivations of liberty in the correctional system. More and more jurists and behavioral scientists feel dubious about the deterrent effects of a prison sentence. The concept of deterrence is based on the idea of a calculating human being, who in a certain situation weighs the advantages of an act against the risks of detection and punishment. This situation simply does not hold for most of the traditional crimes involving violence and property. In addition, KRUM is of the opinion that norms necessary to human coexistence cannot be created by threats of punishment; the logical consequence of general prevention as grounds for the deprivation of liberty in a class society is

---

*Adapted from the National Swedish Association for Penal Reform, 1972. KRUM is a private Swedish organization.

to make members of the lowest social strata serve as a warning example to others.

KRUM rejects the treatment ideology as a basis for restraints on individual liberty. In KRUM's opinion no meaningful treatment can be given on the basis of a coercive deprivation of liberty, and the idea of institutional care has done no more than legitimatize the society's control policy. Moreover, owing to the prognostic way of thinking associated with the treatment ideology, offenders from the lowest social strata are punished more severely than offenders from the higher strata.

The resocialization effect imputed to deprivation of liberty is contradicted by various factors, among them the high rate of recidivism at the prisons. It is a paradox that the one who is supposed to become readjusted to the standards of society should be screened off as effectively as possible from that society.

Lastly, regarding the alleged need to incarcerate certain dangerous offenders, the danger they pose as well as their numbers have been strongly overemphasized in the penology debate. To incarcerate an individual on grounds of protecting the society, moreover, is merely to push the problem aside rather than try to solve it: After all, the individual does not stay in prison forever. And by parting with the deprivation of liberty as a means of protecting society, one will be compelling oneself to look for new and more humane forms of social control.

History

KRUM was founded by social workers, jurists, journalists, convicted offenders, and others at the so-called Thieves' Parliament in the autumn of 1966. One of KRUM's first steps was to criticize the plans to erect a number of modern, completely closed *industrial* prisons. The penology debate was stirred up in the mass media, and the *Kumla series* (so called after the prison of that name) is no longer being built, at least not for the time being.

KRUM sought from the outset to humanize the correctional system. Demands were put forth to improve arrangements for visiting prisons, to grant more leaves, to do away with the censorship of letters, to strengthen noninstitutional care, and so on. But after a couple of years, KRUM began to extend its criticism to the whole of penology, considered within the context of public policy. Internal changes in the prisons were no longer thought to suffice; instead, the very existence of prisons was questioned. However, KRUM did not abandon its earlier demands but preferred to lend active support to the prisoners and their representative councils in their struggle for improved prison conditions.

KRUM also cooperates with other organizations and, during the past two years or so especially, with three other *R bodies* RMH, RFHL and RFMT (the national associations for mental health, help to drug abusers, and environmental therapy, respectively). This cooperation may be seen as an example of KRUM's broadened horizon. All these associations contain individuals whose *deviation* has resulted from society's alienating mechanisms. Society then tries to cure these symptoms by requiring custody at different types of institutions.

Manifestations and Actions

KRUM's activities may be divided into study programs, opinion-molding, and contacts. Under a joint arrangement with the Workers' Educational Association (ABF), KRUM runs study circles on penology all over Sweden. For opinion-molding purposes KRUM has organized a great many conferences and debates at the local, as well as national, level. A couple of the conferences have been documented in book form. In connection with visits and discussion groups at the prisons, the members of KRUM inform themselves about the conditions and demands of the inmates to make them better known to the community at large. Among other actions that KRUM has undertaken, mention may be made of the following:

REPRESENTATIVE COUNCILS: Beyond doubt one of the most important issues for KRUM has been to encourage the formation of organization at the prisons. In the spring of 1969 KRUM dispatched a circular to all institutions urging them to let the prisoners form representative councils. At present about half the institutions have such councils.

STRIKES AND NEGOTIATIONS: Efforts by the prison authorities to frustrate the work of the representative councils have given rise to labor and hunger strikes at the institutions. In these situations the headquarters of KRUM in Stockholm, with the assistance of its local chapters, has been able to function as a center of liaison and information. KRUM has provided the prisoners with expert legal and psychological service in their negotiations with the National Correctional Administration.

PRISON NEWSPAPERS: KRUM's local chapters help to distribute and sell prison newspapers to the general public.

CONTACTS BY MAIL: KRUM has arranged correspondence contacts for at least 1,000 prisoners (questionnaire surveys carried out at different prisons have shown that more than 50 percent of all prisoners never receive a letter or a visit).

PROBATION OFFICERS: KRUM also tries to recruit voluntary probation officers.

PUBLICATIONS: KRUM puts out a house organ called "Krumbukt." In partnership with the other *R* associations, KRUM also publishes the periodical, "R," which comes out six times a year in pocketbook form.

The Organization of KRUM

KRUM now has some 8,000 members, roughly half of them having been imprisoned. Members are organized in about ten local chapters. Each chapter is an autonomous entity responsible for its own activities. The national association performs an advisory function and is called upon to coordinate actions and disseminate information to the local chapters, the prisons, and mass media. Representatives of the prisons, as well as of the local chapters, sit on the KRUM Board, which meets approximately once every two months. KRUM finances its activities from membership dues and an annual government grant of about $7,200.

APPENDIX B

REGULATIONS FOR THE EXPERIMENT ON PAYING WORK EARNINGS ADJUSTED TO OPEN MARKET RATES TO INMATES AT TILLBERGA PRISON*

THE PURPOSE OF THE EXPERIMENT at Tillberga is to extend the opportunities for inmates sentenced to imprisonment to work under conditions similar to those in the open labor market. The higher payment is to be used to improve the inmates' financial and social situation in preparation for release.

The National Correctional Administration has issued the following special regulations to apply to the experiment with rates of payment adjusted to market levels. In addition to these special regulations reference can be made to those in Circular No. 2, 1968, and to directions for treatment given elsewhere. The present regulations take effect on a date to be announced by the National Correctional Administration in a special directive and will apply up to and including March 31, 1973. Regulations for the period after that date will be issued by the administration on the basis of experience gained.

1. *PARTICIPANTS*

To be eligible for participation in the experiment, an inmate must be

a. sentenced to imprisonment;
b. suitable for placement at an open institution;
c. in good health, fit for work, and interested in industrial work; and
d. willing, in active cooperation with the staff, to put his finances in order before being released.

An inmate who wishes to take part in the experiment shall acquaint himself with the regulations for it and agree to the condi-

*Adapted from the National Swedish Correctional Administration Circular No. 4, 1972.

tions laid down. He shall then make a personal application for placement at Tillberga.

Decisions on placement will be made by the eastern regional director.

If special reasons require it, an inmate shall be medically examined before any decision on placement at Tillberga is made.

2. *TRANSFER*

An inmate who clearly shows lack of work effort, who knowingly gives false information in connection with efforts to straighten out his finances, or who acts in some other way that is clearly contrary to the purpose of the experiment may be excluded from further participation.

An inmate who, because of accident or illness, is expected to be unfit for work for more than two weeks may be temporarily transferred from the institution. Any inmate who has been forced to go out of the experiment for this reason shall, as soon as he is fit, be given priority for his return to the institution.

3. *FURLOUGH*

Regarding the purpose of the experiment and the demands made on the participants, the administration, on the basis of § 98, para. 2 of the Treatment Circular, authorizes the granting of a furlough once a month in addition to the regular or special furloughs provided for in § 99, points 1-6 of the Treatment Circular. This additional furlough (Tillberga furlough) may be granted beginning in the second month at Tillberga. Otherwise, the rules for government furlough in the Correctional Circular are applicable.

Tillberga furloughs may only be granted for the time after work on Friday afternoon until 10 P.M. Sunday evening, and travel time should be included.

In general, the Tillberga furlough may not be split up or combined with some other furlough. The governor of the prison may make exceptions to this rule in special cases.

4. *GENERAL REGULATIONS ON REMUNERATION*

Payment is made to inmates who, during working hours, take part in one of the following activities:

4.1 PRACTICAL WORK

By practical work is meant work in the engineering shop or in the factory producing prefabricated wooden houses, and cleaning work.

4.2 SPECIAL ACTIVITIES

Special activities mean appearances before the treatment or supervisory board and attendance at meetings of consultative bodies, as well as the inmate council.

5. *TYPES OF EARNINGS AND PRINCIPLES FOR CALCULATION*

Earnings take the following forms:

5.1 WORK REMUNERATION

Work remuneration is payment for fully completed work output and only for work which has been approved. Any errors or faults caused by an inmate are to be corrected by him without pay, unless special circumstances give reason for some other decision.

5.1.1 Payment for Piecework

Work remuneration is normally based on output and calculated from piecework rates for individuals or groups.

Schedules of rates payable for individual and group piecework are set by the Correctional Administration. The schedules are made available to the inmates.

Payments for piecework must be debited to the account for the branch of operations or the budgetary appropriation to which the work is related.

5.1.2 Time Rates

Work remuneration may be calculated on a time-rate basis only for work performed during a learning period and work for which piece rates cannot be set. The learning period should not exceed three weeks.

Time-rate payments must be debited to the account for the branch of operations or the budgetary appropriation to which the work is related.

5.1.3 Remuneration in the Case of Unavoidable Work Stoppage

Work is remunerated when unavoidable work stoppages lasting at least thirty minutes occur if the cause is a power failure, the breakdown of a machine or some comparable trouble, inclement weather, or other conditions preventing work, providing that the inmate has not at that time been allotted other work.

The payment must be debited to the account for the process in which the stoppage occurs.

5.1.4 Payment for Overtime Work

Overtime payment is made for work which an inmate is instructed to perform outside his normal working hours.

If the work is carried out during hours when the inmate would otherwise not be at work, overtime payment shall consist of a 50-percent addition to the wage that is normally paid.

Overtime payments must be debited to the account for the operation in which the overtime is performed.

5.2. SPECIAL PAYMENTS

5.2.1 Special Activities

Payment is made for participation in the special activities listed under 4.2. Payment is fixed at an hourly rate. Payments must be debited to the account for special activities. (No. 528 112-6).

5.2.2 Sickness and Accident

Sick pay is given to an inmate who, as the result of illness or accident, is put on the sick-list by the institution's doctor or by one of the medical staff and who for that reason incurs the loss of some other form of payment. Sick pay begins on the day following the occurrence of the illness or accident and is set at a fixed rate per workday. If the inmate is transferred from the institution because of the illness or accident, sick pay is given in accordance with the regulations in Circular No. 4, 1971.

Sick pay is to be debited to the account for medical care and treatment.

5.2.3 Reward Payments

Reward payments may be made to an inmate who carries out work of special value for correctional handling or who does something particularly praiseworthy such as suggesting a more rational method of production, preventing an accident, or intervening, when an accident is about to occur.

Any proposal for a reward payment must be made to the National Correctional Administration through the prison governor.

6. *REMUNERATION AMOUNTS*

The amount for the different types of payment will be made available to workers.

7. *APPORTIONMENT OF EARNINGS*

7.1 DEDUCTION FOR FOOD

Inmates shall pay the same prices for meals as correctional personnel. Deductions for meals eaten on days that are ordinary workdays in the workshops are to be made on each payday. No deduction is to be made for days an inmate is registered as sick.

No deduction for food is to be made for days an inmate spends outside the institution on furlough, on the condition that, in accordance with rules set by the management of the institution, the inmate signs a special list indicating that he will not be eating in the dining hall.

7.2 SPENDING MONEY

The inmate may freely dispose of 25 percent of his pay remaining after food deductions have been made. However, of the first two payments received while at Tillberga, an inmate may freely dispose of 50 percent.

7.3 REMAINING MONIES

The amount of an inmate's wages remaining when he has paid for his food and received his pocket money shall be used to improve his financial and social situation in preparation for release.

8. *BUDGET PLANNING*

In consultation with the staff each inmate shall set up a budget which must be confirmed by the directing staff of the institution. Except in cases where it is obviously unnecessary, a copy of the budget is to be sent to the probation officer in the district where the inmate will live after being released.

Inmates shall be encouraged to make personal contact with their creditors and the public authorities in order to reach agreement about the regulation of their debts.

APPENDIX C

REPORT ON AN EXPERIMENT WITH THE PAYMENT OF WORK EARNINGS ADJUSTED TO OPEN-MARKET RATES AT TILLBERGA OPEN PRISON*

IN A STUDY MADE IN 1959, the goals of an experiment with the payment of market wages were, *inter alia,* stated to be "improvement of work output of inmates, of their financial circumstances and possibilities for social adjustment, together with a decrease in costs for social welfare and the financial support of the correctional authorities" (SOU 1959:18; *"Fånges arbetsersattning").*

The study also stressed the fact that the system was not applicable to all prison inmates. Should the experiment prove successful, it should be carefully extended by stages to apply to wider groups of inmates.

Between 1965 and 1971 further studies were carried out by the Correctional Administration. None of the results at present are available in English, but a summary in Swedish can be found in PM NR 1, November 16, 1971: *"Marknadsmässig ersättning till intagna inom kriminalvarden, Diskussionsunderlag."*

The experiment finally started in November 1972. The present report gives an account of various matters concerning the experiment and briefly presents the regulations issued for it. The complete set of regulations is available in English in Circular No. 4, 1972, "Regulations for the experiment on paying work earnings adjusted to open-market rates to inmates at Tillberga prison."

One of the conditions of the experiment is that the system of market wages is applied to all inmates in the experimental prison regardless of their respective types of work. The rates are set in accordance with existing collective labor agreements. At Tillberga wood and engineering industrial work is undertaken, as well as support and maintenance work in the kitchen and the living units.

*Adapted from the National Swedish Correctional Administration, Work and Education Department, 1973.

Thus, several different labor agreements could be used for setting the rates, but as most of the inmates (75 percent) work in the wood industry, agreements and statistics from the wood industry are used as a basis for setting all rates for factory work. Maintenance work is paid under a contract which is also adjusted to the factory rates.

Among the central questions connected with rate setting are those of taxation and compensation in case of illness or accident.

The question of taxation has turned out to be very complex. Intensive discussions inside the National Correctional Administration, as well as with other governmental departments, so far have only led to a temporary solution. If the system with market wages is successful enough to be extended and made a permanent feature of the correctional system the taxation question will have to be thoroughly analyzed in cooperation with other state authorities to make a definitive solution possible. For the present experimental period taxation is computed by a simple, general deduction. The percentage of deduction (32%) is the same for all inmates and is included in the rate setting. This means that the earnings paid correspond approximately to the net wages of an ordinary worker. This simplified method saves much administration.

As no income is formally reported and no contributions are made to the social insurance, the inmates receive no benefits in case of illness or accident. Instead, the prison pays a compensation calculated on the average income during the two weeks preceding the illness.

The Correctional Administration has given special attention to the rules regulating the use of earnings. These matters are considered to be of great importance because of the possibility of improving the financial and social situation of the inmates during their imprisonment.

Inmates do not pay lodging costs but do pay the actual cost of their meals.

The aim of the experiment is a long-range improvement of the releasing situation. But to stimulate interest for application to Tillberga, the amount which inmates may have for their immediate personal use is somewhat larger than that authorized in other prisons. It has been set at 25 percent of the earnings.

The rest of the remuneration, after deduction for meals and immediate use, is divided up in accordance with an individual budgetary plan. The budgetary plan is made up by the inmate together with an assistant from the prison staff. In the budgetary work the whole social and financial background of the inmate must be considered. For those participants in the Tillberga experiment having large debts of different kinds, it is necessary to decide in which order and to what extent the debts are to be repaid. It has proved impossible to give general directions. Each case must be treated individually. The Correctional Administration has recommended that certain types of debts, i.e. unpaid fines, be paid first, since these types of debts are likely to cause much trouble immediately after release. Even when it is not possible to pay off all the debts during the period of imprisonment, an installment plan can often be made up for a longer period of time and can be continued after release. In some cases, however, it may seem more urgent to retain rights to some property by payments, e.g. the rent of a flat. An important factor is the length of the imprisonment. For short-termers the need for cash on release can be the most important matter. For all inmates, a certain amount is set aside for the release, with the result that most inmates have some $144 or more on release. Those with no large debts may have notably more, but in such cases part of the amount is sent to the probation supervisor to be managed by him.

As to the number of allowed furloughs, the Correctional Administration has decided on a considerable increase, with regard to the high demands made on behavior and work achievements of the inmates. Apart from the regular furloughs, inmates at Tillberga get a special monthly leave from their second month on. This special leave is from Friday afternoon until Sunday night so as not to interfere with the work. This system has turned out extraordinarily well. From the start of the experiment until June 30, 1973, 873 furloughs were given. Of these, only twelve (1.4%) have been abused. The generous furloughs have considerably improved the spirit at the institution, as well as the inmates' contacts with the outside world. This part of the experiment has proved a good influence in itself and deserves special notice. The system has now been further extended, and instead of regular furloughs the special

Tillberga leave is granted every second week.

The selection of the participants is probably an important cause of the good result. During the first part of the experiment, no prison inmates sentenced to internment or youth prison were admitted to Tillberga. More recently, however, such inmates can, in principle, be admitted.

The inmate himself fills out an application form, on which he lists his social and financial situation. On the basis of this application form and other relevant data, the decision for acceptance is made by a small group consisting of two representatives from the prison and one psychologist. Where necessary, the psychologist has personal contact with the applicant before the decision is made. So far, less than half of all applicants have been accepted. The general opinion among the prison staff is that the choice has resulted in a notably better clientele in the prison. The inmates are said to be more concerned about their work tasks and to take more part in organized activities during their leisure time. The very few misused furloughs also suggest that it is an elite clientele at the prison and that this may have a significant influence on the good results of the experiment.

Of those applicants who have been refused, the most common reason has been drug abuse or lack of the stability needed for this very open type of prison with its high demands on behavior and work capacity.

Information and education of prison staff and inmates have played an important part in the experiment. Folders are available to the inmates at most prisons to inform them of the experiment and to stimulate them to apply for participation. Prison staffs and probation officers have also been informed. At the beginning of the experiment, there were some doubts among the staff at Tillberga, but as the experiment has proceeded, interest and enthusiasm have risen among all categories of personnel. The positive attitudes of the personnel are also important for the success of the experiment. Continuing training is given to inmates through seminars and courses on financial and social matters. A videotape has been produced which takes up questions concerning inmates' financial problems and possible solutions. The videotape is used as a basis for staff and inmate discussions both in Tillberga and other prisons.

The Correctional Administration is well aware that information cannot be given on a once-for-all basis. The turnover of the prison clientele is very large, and thus, the prisons must constantly receive information. Additional materials are being worked out for this purpose.

The inmates have been overwhelmingly in favor of the experiment giving a most positive response before, as well as during, the experiment. The interaction between the inmates and prison and project leaders has worked out well, largely due to the inmates' own organization, "Club Futura." Club Futura takes an active part in the life at the prison, and many of its suggestions have been carried out in practice.

The Correctional Administration has taken steps to gather information about the participants. Apart from ordinary statistics on wages, facts about the participants have been taken from their application forms, treatment journals, medical cards, and interviews. The collected information is to be used for a short-range evaluation of the activities in the prison, as well as for a subsequent long-range evaluation involving a follow-up after release. It has already been found that the time for individual counseling on social and financial matters is too limited. Far more time is required for this than was originally foreseen. In addition to the written data, information is obtained by interviewing inmates on release. During the period covered by this report, sixty-two inmates have been interviewed, and indications can be found as to what the inmates have appreciated. The furloughs are mentioned as the foremost asset at Tillberga. They have made it possible for the inmates to keep up normal social contacts with their families and the outside world. In this connection it is to be noticed that the market wages are an essential prerequisite for the many furloughs since the inmates have paid the cost of their furloughs themselves. The interviews have also shown that the long visiting hours—six every Sunday—are very popular. In most cases this selected clientele has a favorable releasing situation with the family, home, and work. The Tillberga system has helped to preserve the good condition, and the inmates subjectively judge their chances to manage freedom as very good.

The inmates do, however, criticize the parole system and complain of a lack of support from the supervisors and the probation officers. In many cases, they have received no visits from representatives for the probation authorities before their release. Inmates also assert that there is a lack of individual psychological treatment, probably because their contacts with the assistants in the prison are centered mostly on financial matters.

It must, however, be stressed again that the material is too sparse and the period of time too short to allow for any far-reaching conclusions. Preliminary contacts have shown that most of the sixty-two that have been released are still at work. Four have relapsed into crime. Only a few have continued to pay their debts according to their budgetary plans. Probation officials have revealed that they feel a need for more information about Tillberga. The written information will probably have to be complemented by personal information in order to lessen the common gap between inmates and representatives in the treatment of the former as free men.

Several other factors have also been investigated. The results will be evaluated and presented in separate research reports.

The changes in the factory production have also been analyzed. In the engineering industry, there has been an increase of 26 percent. In the manufacture of prefabricated houses, no direct comparison can be made because the production methods and the bases for rate fixing have been changed. Subjectively judged, however, there has been a production increase which is also attested to by the factory foremen.

The experience gained during the first ten months of the experiment cannot yet form the basis of any conclusions as to whether market wages can be introduced on a large scale. The Tillberga system places high demands on the participants. Realistically, only a limited number of inmates can stand up to these demands. But for those who can manage a normal work output and the relative freedom of the Tillberga system, this probably offers the best alternative for carrying out a prison sentence at present. To judge the results fairly the Tillberga experiment should be continued and preferably extended to some other prison, perhaps a closed type. Not for a much longer time can any definite evaluation be made, but at present many facts suggest that an important new step in corrections has been taken through the Tillberga experiment.

INDEX

143